Spiritual Gifts, Plain and Simple

Spiritual Gifts,

Plain and Simple

Discovering Which

One You Possess

and How to

Maximize It

James D. Wise

VMI Publishers • Sisters, Oregon

The author would like to acknowledge, Network: Participant's Guide, for it's invaluable guidance in defining some of the spiritual gifts discussed in this book. Network: Participant's Guide, Copyright © 1994 by Willow Creek Community Church. Requests for information should be addressed to: Zondervan, Grand Rapids, Michigan 49530.

Published by
VMI Publishers
Sisters, Oregon
www.vmipublishers.com

ISBN: 1933204648

ISBN 13: 9781933204642

Library of Congress Control Number: 2008924931

Printed in the USA

Cover design by Joe Bailen

Table of Contents

Introduction

A recent search on Amazon.com for books on "spiritual gifts" returned 123,839 matches. That's a lot of books on one topic, so the relevant question becomes: "Does the church need someone to write the 123,840th book on this subject?"

Not long ago I was listening to a sermon on the spiritual gifts. The preacher said that while there are a large number of spiritual gifts noted in the Scriptures, every Christian has only one. A few months later I heard another minister preaching on this same topic. He stated that every Christian has several spiritual gifts. Confused by this difference of opinion between two respected teachers of God's Word, I went to a pastor I know and asked, "Which is it? Do Christians have only one spiritual gift or do we all have several?"

He explained that since the Holy Spirit is the source of spiritual gifts and the Spirit indwells every Christian, every Christian has the potential to manifest *all* of the spiritual gifts.

By that time, I felt overwhelmed. I had asked the question, hoping I was only responsible for one gift, and thus, one particular area of ministry. Having several gifts just added to the work I assumed I was required to do in the church. Then I find out that not only do I have more than one gift…I have them all! More confusing was the fact that the more reading I did on this subject, the more the number representing "all" became a moving target.

For example, some teachers do not recognize all of the spiritual gifts listed in the Bible as being valid, arguing that some of the gifts were only operative during the time of the apostles. Other equally competent teachers insist that all of the gifts are still operable today. A few teachers focus on just seven gifts, some recognize a dozen or so, others list twenty-something. Still others list more than thirty. I started to think I was better off not knowing.

So back to my original question: Why do we need yet another book on spiritual gifts? From my perspective the answer is simple. It is because there is a lack of clear teaching on the subject, way too much disagreement among the teachers, and a failure by most to recognize a clear distinction—or "grouping"—of the spiritual gifts as taught in the New Testament. Consider the following passage in which the apostle Paul begins to teach on this important subject:

> Now about spiritual gifts, brothers, I do not want you to be ignorant…There are different kinds of *gifts,* but the same Spirit. There are different kinds of *service,* but the same Lord. There are different kinds of *working,* but the same God works all of them in all men (1 Cor. 12:1, 4–6 italics mine).

In this book I hope to impart a clear—and wholly biblical—understanding of spiritual gifts. In order to gain such an understanding, we must see the natural grouping of the gifts as taught in God's Word. We'll see that each particular grouping of gifts is attributed to a different member of the Trinity. I'll explain why some of the spiritual gifts commonly listed in this type of Bible study are not spiritual gifts at all. We'll discuss why it is possible for a Christian to manifest a particular gift once or twice and then never experience that gift again. Finally, we'll discover that every Christian has one particular gift, given directly by God the Father to serve as our underlying motivation for every area of ministry service. It is this "motivational" gift of the Father that leads to passionate and joyful service in the church and enables us to bear abundant fruit.

For the majority of folks reading this book, it is possible that what I'm teaching will conflict somewhat with what you've learned in the past. All I ask is that you read with an open mind and hold everything I say up to the light of God's Word.

This book will not eliminate the confusion or controversy associated with this topic. Great theologians have disagreed for ages about such topics as baptism (sprinkle or dunk, baptize or dedicate infants), predestination (God's sovereign choice or man's free will), creation (a literal six days or a much longer period) and the role of women in the church. Similarly, I suspect the debate over spiritual gifts will continue until Jesus returns for His bride, the church.

My purpose in writing, then, is not to try and end the debate but to equip the saints. God has given us spiritual gifts for the building up of the body of Christ. Our gifts are to be exercised (1 Tim. 4:14), developed (2 Tim. 1:6) and used in service to Christ's church (1 Pet. 4:10). If we are to be obedient and fulfill our unique role in advancing God's agenda in the world, we must be able to identify our area of spiritual giftedness. Only then can we "run with perseverance the race marked out for us" (Heb. 12:1) so that, at the end of our days, we can proclaim with the apostle Paul that "I have fought the good fight, I have finished the race, I have kept the faith" (2 Tim. 4:7).

We are all called to serve in the church, to give ourselves wholeheartedly to the cause of Christ. The starting point for this service is to identify and cultivate the spiritual gift God has given us to enable that service. Only then can each of us confidently serve in the ministry area that we were meant to serve in, and only then will our service bear abundant fruit for the glory of Jesus our Lord.

Chapter One

Why Am I So Confused?

"But in fact God has arranged the parts in the body, every one of them, just as he wanted them to be."

1 Corinthians 12:18

Studying the spiritual gifts can be frustrating for many folks because the list of gifts tends to change from one teacher to another. As noted in the introduction, some teachers believe that certain of the gifts ceased to be operable after the closing of the New Testament canon. Others disagree, finding no evidence in the Scriptures for this position and concluding therefore that all of the gifts continue in operation today. Some teachers focus on a list of just seven spiritual gifts, some find in the Scriptures twenty-one specific gifts, and others a list in excess of thirty.

Similarly, some pastors teach that every Christian has a single spiritual gift, some believe that every Christian has every gift, and many take a position in between; i.e., that each Christian has at least one or two primary gifts and multiple secondary gifts. I wondered how there could be so much confusion and disagreement over what seemed like a relatively simple concept. This seems like a topic that is important to God, at least when we consider the number of passages that mention spiritual gifts.

Is it unreasonable to believe that God wants us to have a clear understanding of this subject?

When I first began studying spiritual gifts, I was immediately confused by one particular concept. There are several passages in which God seems to be saying that each of us has only one spiritual gift and that we are responsible to identify, develop and exercise this gift. In other passages it appears that we have multiple gifts and at times we won't even know what particular gift we'll be using to contribute to someone's edification. Consider the following:

GIFT SPECIFIED AND SINGULAR:

1 Timothy 4:14	Do not neglect *your gift,* which was given you through a prophetic message when the body of elders laid their hands on you.
2 Timothy 1:6	For this reason I remind you to fan into flame *the gift of God,* which is in you through the laying on of my hands.
1 Peter 4:10	Each one should use *whatever gift* he has received to serve others, faithfully administering God's grace in its various forms.

GIFT UNSPECIFIED AND MULTIPLE:

Romans 1:11–12	I long to see you so that I may impart to you *some spiritual gift* to make you strong—that is, that you and I may be mutually encouraged by each other's faith.
1 Corinthians 12:31	But eagerly desire *the greater gifts.*
1 Corinthians 14:1	Follow the way of love and eagerly desire *spiritual gifts,* especially the gift of prophecy.

The first three passages above seem to imply that each Christian has a particular spiritual gift (singular), given to us at the time of our conversion for the purpose of motivating our service to the body of Christ. The second three passages indicate that we should desire/pursue multiple gifts (plural), that some gifts are greater than others (especially the gift of prophecy) and that we don't always know which gift we'll be using to build someone up in their faith.

The sense of Paul's statement in Romans 1:11 seems to be that the joint exercise of "some" spiritual gift—i.e., a gift that is either unknown or unspecified—will bring mutual edification and encouragement. Conversely, in another epistle he focuses Timothy's attention on one specific gift, a gift that is not to be neglected and which Timothy is to "fan into flame." Different still is his counsel to the Corinthians to desire multiple gifts—"greater gifts"—especially the gift of prophecy. Which is it? Do I have one gift or many? If many, which am I supposed to fan into flame? Should I be content with the gift I'm fanning into flame or should I be pursuing/desiring other gifts?

One Gift or Many?

I decided to begin by compiling a list of spiritual gifts from a number of teachers and commentators. As noted above, there tends to be differences of opinion as to how many spiritual gifts are identified in the Scriptures, but I limited my list to those on which there appeared to be a general consensus. Following is a fairly common list of spiritual gifts:

- Giving
- Leadership
- Encouragement
- Mercy
- Prophecy
- Service
- Teaching
- Administration
- Apostle
- Discernment
- Faith
- Healing
- Helps
- Knowledge
- Miracles
- Speaking in Tongues
- Interpreting Tongues
- Wisdom
- Evangelism
- Pastor
- Celibacy
- Hospitality
- Martyrdom
- Missionary
- Voluntary Poverty
- Intercession
- Craftsmanship
- Music
- Leading Worship

I then decided to look at the life and ministry of two very prominent Christians in the New Testament, men whose involvement in the early church was significant enough for us to be able to identify which spiritual gift or gifts they displayed. The subjects of this review are the apostles Peter and Paul. Before reading on, and based on any current knowledge you have about the ministry of these two men, look at the list above and try to identify the gift or gifts each man displayed in his ministry service.

Let's begin with Peter. The gifts we can be certain he displayed include: leadership (Acts 1, 2, 15); prophecy (Acts 5); teaching (1 Pet.; 2 Pet.); apostle (Matt. 4); discernment (Acts 8); faith (Matt. 14; Luke 9); healing (Acts 3); miracles (Acts 5); evangelism (Acts 2, 3).

As for the apostle Paul, there are likewise a number of gifts he displayed over the course of his ministry: leadership (Acts 11, 15); prophecy (Acts 13); teaching (his epistles); apostle (Rom. 1); healing (Acts 14, 20); miracles (Acts 14, 19); speaking in tongues (1 Cor. 14); evangelism (Acts 13, 14 and other chapters.); celibacy (1 Cor. 7); missionary (Acts 13).

These lists may not be complete, but the conclusion is clear nonetheless: Both apostles displayed any number of different spiritual gifts. Why then do both Peter (1 Pet. 4:10) and Paul (1 Tim. 4:14; 2 Tim. 1:6) encourage us as Christians to identify and exercise our spiritual *gift,* using the term in the singular? The answer, as we'll see in the next few chapters, is that there are actually *different categories* of spiritual gifts.

THREE GENERAL CATEGORIES

In one category of spiritual gifts we might see a particular gift manifest itself through us only one time, never to be repeated. An example of this type of gift in action is in Acts 9:17, where a disciple of the Lord named Ananias placed his hands on Saul of Tarsus and restored his eyesight. There is no evidence of this particular disciple being involved in other healings either before or after this incident.

In the same way, the miracle of raising someone from the dead was rarely seen throughout biblical history. Jesus raised the dead to life (e.g., Luke 7; Luke 8; John 11). And this miracle was also performed through

Elijah (1 Kings 17), Paul (Acts 20) and Peter (Acts 9). But in the case of all three of these men, this particular miracle was a one-time event, never to be repeated through them.

The fact is that there is one particular category of spiritual gifts that cannot be developed or pursued. We might display the gift on multiple occasions or only once, and we often cannot even anticipate or expect to display it in a given situation.

There is another category of gifts that is completely voluntary, that is to say we can pick and choose when and how we will serve within these particular gift areas.

Finally, there is a category of gifts that are dispensed by God the Father Himself, and each of us has been endowed with only one. We didn't choose it and we cannot change it, but we are responsible to identify and cultivate it. This category of gifts is the driving force—the motivation—behind all successful and effective ministry efforts.

We are ready to begin developing the biblical foundation for the study of spiritual gifts, but first I think it will be helpful to narrow the list of gifts a bit. I mentioned earlier that the number of spiritual gifts listed varies widely from one teacher/commentator to another. I've determined that the most significant factor contributing to the discrepancy between teachers involves the inclusion of gifts that, upon close review, are not spiritual gifts at all. The "gifts" in question might be better described as natural talents or acquired skills. Let's deal with this issue in more detail before moving on to our study of the different categories of spiritual gifts.

Chapter Two

Natural Talent, Acquired Skill or Spiritual Gift?

"I have filled him with the Spirit of God, with skill, ability and knowledge in all kinds of crafts."

Exodus 31:3

While most Bible teachers cite the very same group of key passages (Rom. 12; 1 Cor. 12; Eph. 4; 1 Pet. 4) as the foundation for their teaching on spiritual gifts, some arrive at a much larger list of gifts than others. This is the result of looking outside those passages that clearly discuss spiritual gifts and including passages that simply describe either a natural talent or an acquired skill. This thought process is admirable since as Christians we believe that, having been created in God's image, any skill or ability we have is attributable to God's grace. Whether describing a gifted preacher, a skilled craftsman or an extraordinary athlete, we'll often use the term "God-given ability" in order to recognize that God is the source of all ability.

An example of a passage that supports this reasoning is Exodus 31:2–5, in which God says to Moses, "See, I have chosen Bezalel son of Uri, the son of Hur, of the tribe of Judah, and I have filled him with the Spirit of God, with skill, ability and knowledge in all kinds of crafts—to make artistic designs for work in gold, silver and bronze, to cut and set stones, to work in wood, and to engage in all kinds of craftsmanship."

Another passage in which God makes clear that our ability derives from Him is Deuteronomy 8:18, in which He states, "But remember the Lord your God, for it is he who gives you the ability to produce wealth."

While affirming God's grace in the bestowing of our natural skills and abilities, we must take care not to confuse these with the spiritual gifts. The concept of spiritual gifts is unique to the New Testament and is associated with a person's coming to faith in Jesus Christ, at which time he receives the indwelling of the Holy Spirit. Spiritual gifts are given to God's people to enable our ministry and service in the church. For example,

> Each one should use whatever gift he has received to serve others, faithfully administering God's grace in its various forms. (1 Pet. 4:10)

> I long to see you so that I may impart to you some spiritual gift to make you strong—that is, that you and I may be mutually encouraged by each other's faith. (Rom. 1:11–12)

These two passages are clearly referring to the spiritual gifts, as evidenced by both the context and their common use of the same Greek root Word (see below). Surely many Christians have been endowed by God with extraordinary ability in such areas as music, craftsmanship and art. Others have developed these skills through years of hard work and practice. But these abilities, even when being exercised within the church and for the glory of Christ, are different from what the Bible describes as spiritual gifts. According to the *New Bible Dictionary:*[1]

> The term "spiritual gifts" represents the common rendering in English of the Greek neuter plural noun *charismata*...which is related to the noun *charis* (grace); they are the concrete expression *charis,* grace coming to visible effect in word or deed...The purpose of these charismatic gifts is primarily the edification of the whole church, and, secondarily, the conversion of unbelievers.

When discussing the topic of spiritual gifts, then, we must confine our study to passages that, in context, address this specific topic. That is not to say that God can't use our natural skills or abilities to bless others or to lead non-Christians to faith in Christ. I am simply making the point that the Bible draws a clear distinction between spiritual gifts—or "grace" gifts—and other natural talents or acquired skills we might individually possess.

If I hear a Christian vocalist who has an incredible voice and I call her talent a spiritual gift, to what do I ascribe the talent of a gifted, non-Christian vocalist? Or if I say the singer's ability is a spiritual gift because she is using her voice to lead worship, what about the vocalist, also a Christian, who only uses this skill in his vocation? Or what about the non-Christian who sings with equal excellence? All of these are demonstrations of natural ability or acquired skill (or both), but none can be characterized as a spiritual gift. Why? Because God doesn't characterize them in that way, and His Word is our ultimate authority when learning about spiritual gifts.

Eliminating from our list of spiritual gifts those things that God ascribes to natural ability (e.g., tending the flocks, Gen. 47:6; producing wealth, Deut. 8:18; construction, craftsmanship, Exod. 36:1) or acquired skill (e.g., hunting, Gen. 25:27; weaving, Exod. 35:36; singing, 1 Chron. 15:22) will undoubtedly reduce the list of possible gifts to a more manageable number. Equally important, it will leave us to study only those particular spiritual gifts characterized as such by God's Word. Our first step, then, in developing a biblical perspective about the spiritual gifts is to limit our study to those passages in God's Word that clearly discuss this topic.

The Challenge

God not only bestows spiritual gifts upon His people, He also commands us to develop and use these gifts for the building up of His body. "Do not neglect your gift" (1 Tim. 4:14); "fan into flame the gift of God" (2 Tim. 1:6); "each one should use whatever gift he has received to serve others" (1 Pet. 4:10). This being the case, it is incumbent upon God's people to seek to identify the gift He has given an individual in order that we might "fan it into flame."

Most Christians I've spoken with about this topic are quite eager to discover their spiritual gift but have experienced frustration in attempting to do so. The reason is that—as I mentioned in the introduction—there is a good deal of confusion on the subject because of the various theological positions taught.

As a layman (I am certainly not a theologian) I experienced firsthand the frustration of trying to sort through these various positions to discover my gift (or gifts, depending on which position was being studied). Surely our Father, the one who bestows the gifts and commands us to identify and exercise them, does not intend for this confusion to exist.

As I began to consult God's Word in hopes of clearing up the confusion in my own mind, I was greatly encouraged. It became clear very quickly that God's teaching on this subject is not ambiguous, nor is theological training necessary for a proper understanding of the subject. I will begin this study where I began my own: by looking at every Bible passage that explicitly deals with the subject of spiritual gifts.

[1]*New Bible Dictionary,* Second Edition, Tyndale House Publishers

Chapter Three

The Biblical Framework for Spiritual Gifts

"Now about spiritual gifts, brothers, I do not want you to be ignorant."

1 Corinthians 12:1

One of the first things I noticed when studying what others had written concerning the spiritual gifts was that many of the supposed "gifts" listed came from Bible passages that are not even discussing spiritual gifts. Sometimes the passages referenced were simply describing natural talents or abilities (e.g., construction, craftsmanship, weaving, singing); other passages referred to offices in the church (e.g., apostle, pastor); still others included some basic activities that are actually commanded of every Christian (e.g., hospitality, intercession, discernment).

Since there is frequent disagreement among teachers as to how many spiritual gifts there are and how many each of us has, I decided to look for common passages, those that tended to be cited consistently as referring specifically to spiritual gifts. Virtually every theologian, commentator and Bible teacher whose work I consulted began their discussion with the same four passages: Romans 12, 1 Corinthians 12, Ephesians 4 and 1 Peter 4. Each of these passages will be discussed in some detail as our study progresses.

Let's first briefly consider every verse in the New Testament that uses the word *charisma* and then try to determine which of these verses refer explicitly to spiritual gifts, as opposed to another type of gift (e.g., the gift of salvation through Jesus Christ or the gift of God's favor). Following is a list of the seventeen New Testament verses using the word *charisma:*

Romans 1:11–12	I long to see you so that I may impart to you some spiritual gift to make you strong—that is, that you and I may be mutually encouraged by each other's faith.
Romans 5:15	But the gift is not like the trespass. For if the many died by the trespass of the one man, how much more did God's grace and the gift that came by the grace of the one man, Jesus Christ, overflow to the many!
Romans 5:16	Again, the gift of God is not like the result of the one man's sin: The judgment followed one sin and brought condemnation, but the gift followed many trespasses and brought justification.
Romans 6:23	For the wages of sin is death, but the gift of God is eternal life in Christ Jesus our Lord.
Romans 11:29	For God's gifts and his call are irrevocable.
Romans 12:6	We have different gifts, according to the grace given us. If a man's gift is prophesying, let him use it in proportion to his faith.
1 Corinthians 1:7	Therefore you do not lack any spiritual gift as you eagerly wait for our Lord Jesus Christ to be revealed.
1 Corinthians 7:7	I wish that all men were as I am. But each man has his own gift from God; one has this gift, another has that.
1 Corinthians 12:4	There are different kinds of gifts, but the same Spirit.
1 Corinthians 12:9	To another faith by the same Spirit, to another gifts of healing by that one Spirit.

1 Corinthians 12:28	And in the church God has appointed first of all apostles, second prophets, third teachers, then workers of miracles, also those having gifts of healing, those able to help others, those with gifts of administration, and those speaking in different kinds of tongues.
1 Corinthians 12:30	Do all have gifts of healing?
1 Corinthians 12:31	But eagerly desire the greater gifts.
2 Corinthians 1:11	Then many will give thanks on our behalf for the gracious favor granted us in answer to the prayers of many.
1 Timothy 4:14	Do not neglect your gift, which was given you through a prophetic message when the body of elders laid their hands on you.
2 Timothy 1:6	For this reason I remind you to fan into flame the gift of God, which is in you through the laying on of my hands.
1 Peter 4:10	Each one should use whatever gift he has received to serve others, faithfully administering God's grace in its various forms.

If you've studied this subject in the past, you may note that curiously absent from this list is 1 Corinthians 12:1, which says: "Now about spiritual gifts, brothers, I do not want you to be ignorant." It is interesting that the statement Paul makes alerting us that he will now teach on the topic of spiritual gifts uses a different Greek word (*pneumatikos*) than *charisma,* which he uses in most of the other passages.

A brief check of the major Bible translations—The New International Version, the New American Standard Bible, the King James Version and the New King James Version—confirms the translation of *pneumatikos* in this verse (and two others) as "spiritual gifts." Why use a different word if Paul is talking about the same subject?

The literal translation of *pneumatikos* in this verse would be "spiritual matters."[1] As we'll soon see with regard to the word *charisma, pneumatikos* has several definitions and the appropriate translation depends on the context. The definition that applies in this context is "belonging to the Divine Spirit, a. of God the Holy Spirit, b. one who is filled with and governed by the Spirit of God."[2]

Although in different contexts, *pneumatikos* is translated in other ways (i.e. "spiritual thoughts" and "spiritual words" in 1 Corinthians 2:13; "spiritual men" in 1 Corinthians 3:1; "spiritual food" in 1 Corinthians 10:3; "spiritual body" in 1 Corinthians 15:44), it is clear that in the context of 1 Corinthians 12:1, Paul is addressing the general topic of spiritual gifts, both here and in 1 Corinthians 14:1 and 14:12, where *pneumatikos* is also translated "spiritual gifts."

From a laymen's perspective, it is as if Paul begins by addressing the broad topic of spiritual gifts and then moves into a discussion of some specific gifts.

Returning to the seventeen *charisma* passages listed above, although all of these verses use the term *charisma* and refer to a "gift" or "gifts," it is clear that they aren't all referring to the same type of gift. The reason is that the Greek word transliterated *charisma* also has several different definitions.

The second step, then, is to look at the various definitions of *charisma* and determine which one applies specifically to spiritual gifts. *The New American Standard New Testament Greek Lexicon* provides the following definitions for the word *charisma:*

1. favor which one receives without any merit of his own;
2. the gift of divine grace;
3. the gift of faith, knowledge, holiness, virtue;
4. the economy of divine grace, by which the pardon of sin and eternal salvation is appointed to sinners in consideration of the merits of Christ laid hold of by faith;

5. grace or gifts denoting extraordinary powers, distinguishing certain Christians and enabling them to serve the church of Christ, the reception of which is due to the power of divine grace operating on their souls by the Holy Spirit.

It is the last definition that is applicable to Paul's discussion about spiritual gifts in 1 Corinthians 12–14. If we compare these definitions to the seventeen charisma passages listed above, it quickly becomes evident that only ten of them are referring to spiritual gifts as characterized by definition #5.

Another five of these verses (Rom. 5:15; 5:16; 6:23; 11:29; 1 Cor. 1:7) fit definition #4 above in that they refer to the gift of salvation through faith in Christ. In 1 Corinthians 7:7 Paul is talking about his gift of celibacy (or remaining unmarried), which could match either definition #2 or #3 (most likely the latter). The final verse is 2 Corinthians 1:11, which fits with definition #1 as evidenced by *charisma* being translated here as "favor" rather than "gift."

The result of this brief review is that, as we seek to develop a biblical theology of spiritual gifts, we are directed to ten specific *charisma* passages to be considered, to which we can add the three *pneumatikos* verses (1 Cor. 12:1; 14:1; 14:12) universally translated as "spiritual gifts." The list of verses we'll focus on follows:

Charisma verses

Romans 1:11–12	I long to see you so that I may impart to you some spiritual gift to make you strong—that is, that you and I may be mutually encouraged by each other's faith.
Romans 12:6	We have different gifts, according to the grace given us. If a man's gift is prophesying, let him use it in proportion to his faith.
1 Corinthians 12:4	There are different kinds of gifts, but the same Spirit.

1 Corinthians 12:9	To another faith by the same Spirit, to another gifts of healing by that one Spirit.
1 Corinthians 12:28	And in the church God has appointed first of all apostles, second prophets, third teachers, then workers of miracles, also those having gifts of healing, those able to help others, those with gifts of administration, and those speaking in different kinds of tongues.
1 Corinthians 12:30	Do all have gifts of healing?
1 Corinthians 12:31	But eagerly desire the greater gifts.
1 Timothy 4:14	Do not neglect your gift, which was given you through a prophetic message when the body of elders laid their hands on you.
2 Timothy 1:6	For this reason I remind you to fan into flame the gift of God, which is in you through the laying on of my hands.
1 Peter 4:10	Each one should use whatever gift he has received to serve others, faithfully administering God's grace in its various forms.

PNEUMATIKOS VERSES

1 Corinthians 12:1	Now about spiritual gifts, brothers, I do not want you to be ignorant.
1 Corinthians 14:1	Follow the way of love and eagerly desire spiritual gifts, especially the gift of prophecy.
1 Corinthians 14:12	Since you are eager to have spiritual gifts, try to excel in gifts that build up the church.

The third step in this process is to determine whether any of these passages is foundational; i.e., whether any passage seeks to explicitly teach doctrine with regard to this subject as opposed to simply mentioning spiritual gifts in passing. Perhaps a few examples will explain my reasoning for this approach.

If we were to commit to studying spiritual warfare, the foundational passage for our study would probably be Ephesians 6:10–20. Although Satan and his attacks are mentioned in many New Testament books, this passage in Ephesians was explicitly written to prepare God's people to take a "stand against the devil's schemes." We wouldn't confine our study solely to this one passage, but this passage would form the foundation of our study and other passages would provide support.

Similarly, were we to study what Christ's church is supposed to look like, we might choose Acts 2:42–47 as our foundational text. Surely there are instructions and warnings for Christ's church throughout the New Testament, but this passage in Acts is generally viewed as a key description of what the church should look like.

If we want to learn how to give our Christian testimony, we might use as our guide Paul's preaching in the meeting of the Areopagus in Acts 17; to understand why Jesus came and died we might begin with Jesus' interaction with Nicodemus in John 3; to understand temptation we should begin with the temptation of Jesus in the wilderness (Matt. 4:1–11; Luke 4:1–13). In all of these cases we would certainly consider the other Bible passages that deal with the same issue, but the texts cited would likely provide the foundation for our study.

If you look back at the thirteen verses that discuss the spiritual gifts, is there one that jumps out at you as being a foundational verse? How about 1 Corinthians 12:1: "Now concerning spiritual gifts, brethren, I do not want you to be unaware" (nasb). If we're looking for a key passage to begin to understand God's teaching on spiritual gifts, my vote is that we begin with the passage in which the apostle Paul explicitly states that this is what he's about to teach us.

This verse will lead us to a more thorough look at 1 Corinthians 12, and even a cursory review of this chapter makes clear that we've located our foundational text. Paul is going to teach us about the spiritual gifts. Why? Because he doesn't want us to be ignorant about this important topic. It is important to God, and should be important to us.

God gave spiritual gifts to the church for a reason. His Word makes clear that these gifts are given for the purpose of building up the body of Christ (1 Pet. 4:10). These gifts are to be discovered and exercised (Rom. 1:11); they are to be "fanned into flame" as Paul instructed Timothy (2 Tim. 1:6). They are not to be neglected (1 Tim. 4:14).

I dare say that this study, if followed through to completion, will transform your personal ministry and, through your ministry, impact countless lives for Christ. I am passionate about this topic, about the vital importance of every Christian discovering and exercising his or her spiritual gift. I hope this chapter has provided the foundation for our study. Now let's begin to build upon it.

[1]The *Interlinear NASB-NIV Parallel New Testament in Greek and English,* Copyright 1993, Zondervan Publishing House.

[2]*New Testament Greek Lexicon,* StudyLight.org

Chapter Four

The Evidence for Grouping Spiritual Gifts

"There are different kinds of gifts, but the same Spirit. There are different kinds of service, but the same Lord. There are different kinds of working, but the same God works all of them in all men."

1 Corinthians 12:4–6

Now that we've identified 1 Corinthians 12 as the foundational text for learning about spiritual gifts, let's look within this passage to discern the key principles being communicated by the apostle Paul. Since the first eleven verses of 1 Corinthians 12 lay the groundwork for understanding spiritual gifts, let's read this section in its entirety before proceeding.

> [1]Now about spiritual gifts, brothers, I do not want you to be igno-
> rant. [2]You know that when you were pagans, somehow or other
> you were influenced and led astray to mute idols. [3]Therefore I tell
> you that no one who is speaking by the Spirit of God says, "Jesus
> be cursed," and no one can say, "Jesus is Lord," except by the Holy
> Spirit. [4]There are different kinds of gifts, but the same Spirit.
> [5]There are different kinds of service, but the same Lord. [6]There are
> different kinds of working, but the same God works all of them in
> all men. [7]Now to each one the manifestation of the Spirit is given
> for the common good. [8]To one there is given through the Spirit
> the message of wisdom, to another the message of knowledge by
> means of the same Spirit, [9]to another faith by the same Spirit, to
> another gifts of healing by that one Spirit, [10]to another miraculous

powers, to another prophecy, to another distinguishing between spirits, to another speaking in different kinds of tongues, and to still another the interpretation of tongues. [11]All these are the work of one and the same Spirit, and he gives them to each one, just as he determines.

THE CONFLICT AT CORINTH

Let's quickly review the reason that Paul thought it necessary to explain the doctrine of spiritual gifts to the church at Corinth, and by extension to the church universal. Paul's letter was written primarily in response to two significant issues that had arisen in this church.

The first involved two problematic reports Paul received concerning the church at Corinth. One of these reports was brought to Paul by members of Chloe's household (1 Cor. 1:11), noting several factions that had arisen in the church; others who had come alerted Paul to a case involving gross immorality that was taking place in the church.

The second issue being addressed in this letter was a request from the church for Paul's counsel on several important doctrinal matters. Specifically, Paul was asked to explain God's position with regard to marriage (7:1), food sacrificed to idols (8:1), spiritual gifts (12:1) and the offering being taken in the churches for their fellow Christians in need at Jerusalem (16:1).

What exactly was the problem this church was experiencing with regard to spiritual gifts? John Calvin, in his commentary on 1 Corinthians, notes: "He [Paul] goes on to correct another fault. As the Corinthians abused the gifts of God for ostentation and show, and love was little, if at all, regarded, he shows them for what purpose believers are adorned by God with spiritual gifts—for the edification of their brethren." Adds Greg Herrick, PhD, in *The Argument of 1Corinthians 12–14*: "From the text of 1 Corinthians 12–14 (and certain other passages) we can create with some degree of accuracy, it would appear, the problem in the Corinthian church...Paul's response reveals that it is a problem with the gift of tongues and the nature of true spirituality. The Corinthians had made the gift of tongues the sign of true spirituality and had urged all to speak in tongues as evidence of such spirituality."

Many of the new Christians at Corinth had come to believe that true spirituality was evidenced only by speaking in tongues. Those in the church who held this belief assumed their brethren who did not speak in tongues either didn't possess the Holy Spirit at all, or at least didn't possess Him to the same degree as those manifesting this particular gift. Paul's first step was to correct this errant perspective. This explains verses 2 and 3, which would otherwise seem out of place in this discussion. Paul says: "You know that when you were pagans, somehow or other you were influenced and led astray to mute idols. Therefore I tell you that no one who is speaking by the Spirit of God says, 'Jesus be cursed,' and no one can say, 'Jesus is Lord,' except by the Holy Spirit" (1 Cor. 12:2–3).

Remember that Paul begins this chapter by stating that he doesn't want the people to be ignorant with regard to spiritual gifts. He immediately reminds them that it is a person's profession of faith that "Jesus is Lord" that provides true evidence of Christianity and of the Holy Spirit's indwelling presence. Likewise he states that anyone who would curse our Lord is not in the Spirit, regardless of any supernatural manifestation he might display. His first point, then, is that we shouldn't judge a person's faith by his spiritual gift but by his profession of faith in Christ as Lord.

The second point Paul makes to correct the Corinthian error is that there are many spiritual gifts that give evidence of the indwelling Holy Spirit, not just the gift of speaking in tongues. That is why he quickly lists other gifts of the Spirit in verses 8–10. The spiritual gift of faith, for example, in a person who follows Jesus is no less important than the gift of speaking in tongues. Nor is it evidence of a lesser or weaker faith. Both gifts come from the Spirit of God, and both are important for the building up of the body.

It is in the midst of this argument that Paul gives the key principle to guide our understanding of spiritual gifts. In verses 4–6 he states: "There are different kinds of gifts, but the same Spirit. There are different kinds of service, but the same Lord. There are different kinds of working, but the same God works all of them in all men." This passage provides the evidence for what I'll call the "grouping" of the spiritual gifts.

UNDERSTANDING THE "GROUPING" OF SPIRITUAL GIFTS

The first thing we should note in verses 4–6 of 1 Corinthians 12 is that all three members of the Trinity (Spirit, Lord, God) are mentioned, each with a specific category of gifts attributed to Him. The second thing we notice is that there are three distinct groupings mentioned within the broad context of spiritual gifts: "gifts," "service" and "working."

Since these three words tend to vary from one translation to another, perhaps it would be helpful to look at this passage in several different translations before going forward. Please note that I am highlighting both the type of gift and the member of the Trinity in each verse for easy identification.

> NEW INTERNATIONAL VERSION: There are different kinds of *gifts,* but the same **Spirit.** There are different kinds of *service,* but the same **Lord.** There are different kinds of *working,* but the same **God** works all of them in all men.

> NEW AMERICAN STANDARD: Now there are varieties of *gifts,* but the same **Spirit.** And there are varieties of *ministries,* and the same **Lord.** There are varieties of *effects,* but the same **God** who works all things in all persons.

> KING JAMES VERSION: Now there are diversities of *gifts,* but the same **Spirit.** And there are differences of *administrations,* but the same **Lord.** And there are diversities of *operations,* but it is the same **God** which worketh all in all.

> NEW KING JAMES VERSION: Now there are diversities of *gifts,* but the same **Spirit.** There are differences of *ministries,* but the same **Lord.** And there are diversities of *activities,* but it is the same **God** who works all in all.

THE ENGLISH STANDARD VERSION: Now there are varieties of *gifts*, but the same **Spirit**; and there are varieties of *service*, but the same **Lord**; and there are varieties of *activities*, but it is the same **God** who empowers them all in everyone.

LITERAL GREEK[1]: Now differences of *gifts* there are, but the same **Spirit**; and differences of *ministries* there are, and the same **Lord**; and differences of *operations* there are, but the same **God** operating all things in all.

Some teachers will summarize this passage by stating there are three kinds of spiritual gifts: gifts of the Father, gifts of the Son and gifts of the Spirit. This is not only biblically accurate, but stating it in this way will help us to easily remember the three groupings. This distinction was the easy one; let's move on to identifying the specific category of spiritual gift attributed to each member of the Godhead. I've found it helpful to differentiate between the gift categories by creating a chart that reflects the terminology used in each translation.

	SPIRIT	LORD	GOD
NIV	gifts	service	working
NASB	gifts	ministries	effects
KJV	gifts	administrations	operations
NKJV	gifts	ministries	activities
ESV	gifts	service	activities
Greek	gifts	ministries	operations

Looking at this list, one point is inescapable: The apostle Paul, under the direct inspiration of the Holy Spirit, is teaching us that there are three different categories of spiritual gifts and that each category is attributable to a different member of the Godhead. If we desire a wholly biblical understanding of this important subject, we must study the spiritual gifts according to their groupings rather than simply lumping all twenty or thirty-plus gifts together in one basket. As we'll see in the next chapter, each category of gift has a specific purpose, and all of the gifts are to be used for the building up of the body of Christ.

Do you know what this reminds me of? The creation of the world. Genesis 1:1 says, "In the beginning **God** created the heavens and the earth." The apostle Paul states in Colossians 1:16, "For by him [**Jesus**] all things were created." Genesis 1:2 notes that "the **Spirit** of God was hovering over the waters." This is a wonderful picture of the Trinity— all three members of the Godhead working together in perfect harmony to accomplish God's purpose in creating the world.

Now we come to His plan for the creation of His church, "built on the foundation of the apostles and prophets, with Christ Jesus himself as the chief cornerstone" (Eph. 2:20). Jesus lives the perfect life and dies the perfect death, opening the door to reconciliation with God. Jesus then rises from the grave and returns to heaven after instructing His followers that the good news of salvation is to be preached to the ends of the earth.

As people respond to the Gospel, repenting of their sins and placing their faith in Jesus, the Holy Spirit indwells the new Christian and endows him or her with spiritual gifts. These gifts are to be exercised by each believer for the purpose of building up Christ's church. Paul states in Ephesians 2:10, "For we are God's workmanship, created in Christ Jesus to do good works, which God prepared in advance for us to do." The spiritual gifts are His means of equipping us for these good works.

There are different categories of gifts and each category applies to every believer. All three members of the Godhead are actively present in the application of these gifts. The next step in our study is to develop an understanding of each category—or grouping—and to determine how God uses each one in the building up of His church.

[1]The *Interlinear NASB-NIV Parallel New Testament in Greek and English*, Copyright 1993, Zondervan Publishing House.

Chapter Five

Gifts of the Spirit: Manifestation Gifts

"Now to each one the manifestation of the Spirit is given for the common good."

1 Corinthians 12:7

Let's turn our attention now to the first of the three groupings of spiritual gifts that Paul mentions in 1 Corinthians 12. In this epistle Paul was particularly concerned with gifts of the Spirit because those gifts were the source of controversy and dissension in the church.

Incidentally, Paul has the same grouping in mind in the Romans 1:11 passage; he looks forward to the sharing of "some" manifestation gift, or gift of the Holy Spirit, between himself and the believers at Rome by which they will encourage one another. The reason the gift is not specified is that there is no way to know in advance the particular way that the Spirit will manifest Himself. Why? Because "all these are the work of one and the same Spirit, and he gives them to each one, *just as he determines*" (1 Cor. 12:11 italics mine).

Just as Paul could not have anticipated his display of the manifestation gift of "miracles" in raising Eutychus from the dead in Acts 20—safe to say he didn't expect someone to fall asleep and then fall out of a window while he was teaching—so he could not know in advance which manifestation gift(s) would be displayed when he met with his brothers and sisters at Rome.

Unlike the gifts of the Father, which we'll discuss in chapter 7, it is important to understand that these gifts of the Spirit cannot be "fanned into flame" because we have no control over them. A gift of the Spirit might manifest itself one time in your life—as needed in a particular situation—and never be seen again. Or the same gift might be seen over and over again as the Spirit wills. This is determined by the Holy Spirit, for He alone knows which gift needs to be manifested in any given situation in order to accomplish His purpose.

Let's look once more at the progression of 1 Corinthians 12:4–7:

> 4There are different kinds of gifts, but the same Spirit. 5There are different kinds of service, but the same Lord. 6There are different kinds of working, but the same God works all of them in all men. 7Now to each one the manifestation of the Spirit is given for the common good.

As you can see, Paul first identifies the three categories of spiritual gifts and then notes which particular group of gifts will be expanded upon. The reason I use the term "manifestation gifts" to describe the gifts of the Spirit is because that is the term Paul uses.

Before listing some of the specific manifestation gifts, however, he makes two points in verse 7 that are necessary in view of the conflict in this church. First, Paul reminds them that the manifestation of the Holy Spirit is given to "each one," meaning each believer in the church in Corinth and, by extension, each believer in the church universal. Remember that some in Corinth with a particular manifestation gift thought more highly of themselves than their brethren, even to the point of questioning whether the Holy Spirit indwelled them at all. Paul refutes this faulty supposition by reminding them that every Christian—"each one"—will manifest the Spirit's presence in some way.

The second point Paul makes is a not-so-subtle reminder that the focus of these manifestation gifts should be the edification of others, not self. These gifts are given "for the common good." The manifestation of a particular gift should never result in spiritual arrogance because it is the Holy Spirit who "gives them to each one, just as he determines" (v. 11).

Nor should there be a condescending self-centeredness, the prideful belief that "my faith is better than your faith" just because I'm more impressed with my manifestation gift than I am with yours. Such an attitude not only dishonors my brothers and sisters who happen to manifest different gifts than I do, it dishonors God the Holy Spirit, the giver of these wonderful gifts.

Having reminded the church that these gifts should not be the cause of division or dissension, Paul goes on to list nine specific manifestation gifts in verses 8–11:

> [8]To one there is given through the Spirit the message of wisdom,
> to another the message of knowledge by means of the same Spirit,
> [9]to another faith by the same Spirit, to another gifts of healing by
> that one Spirit, [10]to another miraculous powers, to another
> prophecy, to another distinguishing between spirits, to another
> speaking in different kinds of tongues, and to still another the
> interpretation of tongues. [11]All these are the work of one and the
> same Spirit, and he gives them to each one, just as he determines.

Among teachers who recognize the three groupings of spiritual gifts there is some question as to whether this represents a partial list of the manifestation gifts or whether the list is complete. This depends on one's opinion as to how many gifts there are; certain "gifts" that don't fall neatly into any of the three categories might generally be grouped with the manifestation gifts by default. Such "gifts" might include discernment, hospitality and intercession, among others. It is my conviction that these "gifts" are not spiritual gifts at all, but rather represent sanctified behavior that is commanded of every Christian. I'll expand on this point in a later chapter.

Whether this list of manifestation gifts is complete is of only secondary importance. Why? Because this grouping of gifts is the work of the Holy Spirit and Him alone; it is not for us to choose our gift or develop it because "all these are the work of one and the same Spirit, and he gives them to each one, just as he determines." While it is helpful to recognize these manifestation gifts and to earnestly seek/desire them, this is not the grouping that God commands us to "fan into flame."

Before moving on to the gifts of the Father and Son, let's summarize what we've learned so far about manifestation gifts. There are several important points to consider that will always apply to the gifts of the Spirit, or manifestation gifts:

1. Manifestation gifts are *given by the Holy Spirit*. In this way they differ from the gifts of the Father (operation/working/activity) and of the Son (service/ministries/administration). (1 Cor. 12:4–6)
2. Manifestation gifts are given to every Christian. (1 Cor. 12:7, 11)
3. Manifestation gifts are given separately to each Christian *as the Holy Spirit determines;* we do not choose which gift or gifts we will manifest. (1 Cor. 12:11)
4. Manifestation gifts are given to each Christian primarily for the *benefit/edification of other Christians*. The person manifesting the gift might also be edified (1 Cor. 14:4), but that is not the primary purpose of these gifts. (1 Cor. 12:7; Rom. 1:11)
5. Manifestation gifts are given by the Holy Spirit as *appropriate to the occasion* or as they are needed to edify/encourage others (Rom. 1:11). Therefore, each Christian is likely to display different manifestation gifts at different times.
6. It is appropriate to *eagerly desire* manifestation gifts but always for the sake of others, not for selfish reasons. (1 Cor. 12:31; 14:1, 12)
7. Manifestation gifts are always and only to be *exercised in love*. (1 Cor. 13:1–13)

Since the primary objective of this study is to help us to identify the singular gift that God commands us to develop and exercise, let us continue our search by examining the gifts of the Son.

CHAPTER SIX

Gifts of the Son: Ministry Gifts

"There are different kinds of service, but the same Lord."

1 CORINTHIANS 12:5

The Greek word *diakonia* used in 1 Corinthians 12:5 is most frequently translated either "service" or "ministry." These ministry gifts represent the various areas of service in Christ's church. They are gifts of the Son, that is, they are Jesus' gifts to His church for the orderly carrying out of His mission.

One of the exciting things about this category of gifts is that, unlike the gifts of the Spirit, which the Holy Spirit chooses for us, we actually get to choose which ministry gifts to use as we determine which area(s) of service are the best fit for us in the local church. The Son is the one who gives the gifts to the church—not to specific individuals. It is actually up to us to determine which ministry gift/gifts is/are the best fit for ourselves.

The most commonly known gifts of the Son are the church offices—e.g., pastor, evangelist, elder, deacon—but any ministry service belongs in this gift category. The primary passage of Scripture referring to this group of gifts is in Ephesians chapter 4:

> 7But to each one of us grace has been given as Christ apportioned it...11It was he who gave some to be apostles, some to be prophets, some to be evangelists, and some to be pastors and teachers, 12to prepare God's people for works of service, so that the

> body of Christ may be built up [13]until we all reach unity in the faith and in the knowledge of the Son of God and become mature, attaining to the whole measure of the fullness of Christ.

As you can see, this particular grouping is attributed to the Lord Jesus (v. 7), and the word translated "grace" here is actually the Greek *charis,* which you might guess is the root of *charisma,* the word most frequently translated "spiritual gifts" in English. The above passage is a continuation of Paul's discussion about our citizenship in Christ's church, "members of God's household, [which is] built on the foundation of the apostles and prophets, with Christ Jesus himself as the chief cornerstone" (Eph. 2:19–20).

The specific ministries, or offices, mentioned above include apostle, prophet, evangelist, pastor and teacher. Note the similarity with 1 Corinthians 12:28–29, where Paul twice mentions three of these same offices (apostles, prophets and teachers). In the Ephesians passage Paul expands the list to include evangelists and pastors, but the term *diakonia* seems used much more broadly in the New Testament than simply describing church offices. In fact, the word is used thirty-four times in the New Testament, and in only a few cases does it refer directly to an office in the church.

The word *diakonia* can be translated several different ways: ministry or ministries; mission; preparations; relief; serve, service or serving; support. Following are the definitions given in *The New Testament Greek Lexicon:*

1. Service, ministering, especially of those who execute the commands of others.
2. Of those who by the command of God proclaim and promote religion among men:
   a. of the office of Moses;
   b. of the office of the apostles and its administrations;
   c. of the office of prophets, evangelists, elders, etc.
3. The ministration of those who render to others the offices of Christian affection, especially those who help meet needs by

either collecting or distributing of charities.

4. The office of deacon in the church.
5. The service of those who prepare and present food.

These definitions might be combined to simply refer to two groups in the church: those who serve in a formal church office and those who support church leadership by serving in various ministries. The best way to understand this category of spiritual gifts is that it answers the question, "Where should I serve?"

Most denominations believe and teach that the offices of evangelist (modern missionaries), elder and deacon, pastor and teacher are perpetual—that is to say these offices will continue to exist until Christ returns for His church.

Likewise, most denominations believe and teach that the offices of apostle and prophet existed only during the first century and ceased to exist once the canon of the New Testament was finalized with the book of Revelation. (I should note, however, that this position is not universally held. This subject will not be debated here as it falls well outside the purpose for which this book was written.)

Examples of ministries that are not church offices are many. Every church has its own unique ministries through which it serves to advance the cause of Christ in its community and around the world. A brief list of such ministries would include:

Greeters
Ushers
Childcare workers
Sunday school teachers
Prayer teams
Worship leaders
Music team
Choir
Sound & AV team
Trustees
Mercy committee
Pulpit committee
Food distribution
Clothing distribution
Care for the elderly
Hospital visitation
Counseling ministry
Youth group leaders
Building and grounds maintenance
Outreach committee
Bereavement ministry
Homeless ministry
Discipleship

These are just some examples, but the ministry gifts of the Son are as various as the needs of the people we are called to serve. As stated in the New American Standard translation: "And there are varieties of ministries, and the same Lord" (1 Cor. 12:5).

Once we've identified the singular spiritual gift each of us has that we are commanded to "fan into flame" (2 Tim. 1:6, see chapter 7 of this book), our next step is to choose a ministry area (or areas) in which to begin exercising that gift. It is a great blessing indeed when we are serving in an area of ministry for which God has uniquely gifted us. That is when we are able to bear much fruit for the kingdom.

As mentioned above, we are free to choose among the gifts of the Son, for all ministry done in His name and for His glory is honoring to our King. Remember that Jesus gave us church officers/leaders in order "to prepare God's people for works of service, so that the body of Christ may be built up until we all reach unity in the faith and in the knowledge of the Son of God and become mature, attaining to the whole measure of the fullness of Christ" (Eph. 4:12–13). The purpose for which our Lord has given us these precious gifts is that we would attain unity and maturity in Him.

Let's conclude this chapter with a few summary points about the second grouping of spiritual gifts, the gifts of the Son:

1. Ministry gifts are given to the church by our Lord Jesus Christ. In this way they differ from the gifts of the Father (operation/working/activity) and of the Spirit. (1 Cor. 12:4–6)
2. Ministry gifts are available to every Christian and represent a variety of different areas of service in the church.
3. Ministry gifts can be divided into two categories: a) church offices, and b) ministry positions that serve to support church leadership in fulfilling the mission of the church.
4. Unlike manifestation gifts, which are distributed by the Holy Spirit as He alone determines, the gifts of the Son are simply areas of ministry in which we choose to serve the church. We are free

to choose among the variety of ministries in our church and may serve in as many as desired.

5. Our diligent exercise of the gifts of the Son will result in the body of Christ being built up, "until we all reach unity in the faith and in the knowledge of the Son of God and become mature, attaining to the whole measure of the fullness of Christ." (Eph. 4:13)

Now we will turn our attention to the category of spiritual gifts that will be the focus of the remainder of this study, the gifts of the Father.

Chapter Seven

Gifts of the Father: Motivational Gifts

"There are different kinds of working, but the same God works all of them in all men."

1 Corinthians 12:6

The Greek word used in 1 Corinthians 12:6, which can be translated either "working," "effects," "activities" or "operation," is *energema*. Note the resemblance to the English word "energy"; this is a good way to understand this term in its context. The spiritual gifts in this particular group represent a direct working—or energy—of God the Father in each of us. Unlike the manifestation gifts of the Spirit, which come and go in the life of each Christian as the Holy Spirit determines, or the ministry gifts of the Son, which we are free to choose as our areas of service to Christ's church, the motivational gift we receive from the Father becomes a permanent part of our spiritual "DNA" at the moment of our conversion (1 Tim. 4:14; 2 Tim. 1:6) and remains throughout our life on earth. This is the singular gift in each believer referred to by both Paul and Peter when they encourage us: "do not neglect your gift" (1 Tim. 4:14); "fan into flame the gift of God" (2 Tim. 1:6); "each one should use whatever gift he has received to serve others" (1 Pet. 4:10).

The reason I use the term "motivational gifts" to describe this grouping is that this working of God in each of us motivates all of our ministry service. A good way to understand this category of spiritual gifts is that it answers the question, "Why do I serve where I serve?"

We can freely choose where to deploy our gift, but we do not choose the spiritual gift that motivates our service; that decision rests with God our Father. Once a person professes faith in Jesus as Savior and the Holy Spirit establishes His indwelling presence (Eph. 1:13–14), God the Father imparts one of the seven motivational gifts to equip the new believer "to do good works, which God prepared in advance for us to do" (Eph. 2:10). This motivational gift is the very operation, or energy, of God the Father at work in each of His children. The New Testament passage that describes this group of gifts is in Romans chapter 12:

> [1]Therefore, I urge you, brothers, in view of God's mercy, to offer your bodies as living sacrifices, holy and pleasing to God—this is your spiritual act of worship. [2]Do not conform any longer to the pattern of this world, but be transformed by the renewing of your mind. Then you will be able to test and approve what God's will is—his good, pleasing and perfect will. [3]For by the grace given me I say to every one of you: Do not think of yourself more highly than you ought, but rather think of yourself with sober judgment, in accordance with the measure of faith God has given you. [4]Just as each of us has one body with many members, and these members do not all have the same function, [5]so in Christ we who are many form one body, and each member belongs to all the others. [6]We have different gifts, according to the grace given us. If a man's gift is prophesying, let him use it in proportion to his faith. [7]If it is serving, let him serve; if it is teaching, let him teach; [8]if it is encouraging, let him encourage; if it is contributing to the needs of others, let him give generously; if it is leadership, let him govern diligently; if it is showing mercy, let him do it cheerfully.

The first thing we might note in this passage is that the gifts listed are attributable to God the Father, unlike those listed in Ephesians 4 (Jesus) and 1 Corinthians 12 (Holy Spirit).

Second, we are to accept our gift as being by grace (v. 6) in accordance with the measure of faith God has given us (v. 3); thus, there is no room for spiritual arrogance (v. 3). None of us is to think or act as if our motivational gift is more important than someone else's. In Christ's church we do not all have the same function, and it is important to understand that a healthy church requires each of its parts to be functioning properly. Each of us belongs to all the others as we exercise our particular motivational gift (v. 5). For this reason we are actually depriving our brothers and sisters in Christ if we fail to exercise our motivational gift. Repeating a common theme, Paul reminds us that these gifts are given, not for our own benefit, but for the building up of the body of Christ.

Paul then goes on to list the seven motivational gifts of God the Father: prophecy, service, teaching, encouragement, giving, leadership and mercy. In the chapters that follow we will look at each of these motivational gifts in detail so that each of us might be able to discern which particular motivational gift God has imparted to us. If you have never discerned your motivational gift, or served in a ministry consistent with your gifting, you will find this discovery process quite liberating. When you understand your motivational gift and fan it into flame, you'll not only serve with greater energy and enthusiasm, but your ministry service will bear abundant fruit (John 15:8; Rom. 7:4).

Two Types of Gift

You may notice that these seven motivational gifts can be broken down into speaking gifts (prophecy, teaching, encouragement) and serving gifts (service, giving, leadership, mercy). This concept seems to be affirmed by Peter in the fourth chapter of his first epistle (emphasis mine):

> [10]Each one should use whatever gift he has received to serve others, faithfully administering God's grace in its various forms. [11]**If anyone speaks,** he should do it as one speaking the very words of God. **If anyone serves,** he should do it with the strength God provides, so that in all things God may be praised through Jesus Christ. To him be the glory and the power for ever and ever. Amen.

You may remember from chapter 3 of this book that 1 Peter 4:10 is one of the four key passages universally agreed to be teaching about spiritual gifts, and it is one of the ten *charisma* passages we identified. Although this passage doesn't mention any specific spiritual gifts, it is clear that Peter is here addressing this third category of gifts, those attributed to God the Father (vv. 10–11). As such, it is appropriate to see this passage as linked to the spiritual gifts noted in Romans 12:6–8.

In referring to the gifts of God the Father, Peter notes that there are *speaking* gifts and *serving* gifts. He also gives us a sober reminder that these gifts are to be administered as if speaking God's words and serving in God's strength. Once again we see that there is no place for spiritual arrogance regarding our motivational gift. The gifts themselves are of God's grace (v. 10), the power to apply them is from God Himself (v. 11), and the purpose of their exercise is God's glory: "so that in all things God may be praised through Jesus Christ" (v. 11).

As we've done with both the gifts of the Spirit and the gifts of the Son, let's conclude this chapter with some summary points that will always apply to the gifts of the Father:

1. Motivational gifts are given by God the Father. They represent a direct energy, operation, activity or working of God the Father in the life of every Christian. In this way they differ from the gifts of the Spirit (1 Cor. 12) and the gifts of the Son (Eph. 4).
2. There are seven motivational gifts, and every Christian is endowed with only one. This gift is not to be neglected (1 Tim. 4:14) and it is to be "fanned into flame" (2 Tim. 1:6).
3. Motivational gifts can be divided into two categories: a) speaking gifts (prophecy, teaching, encouragement), and b) serving gifts (service, giving, leadership, mercy).
4. As with the manifestation gifts and ministry gifts, we are to exercise our motivational gift in service to—and for the benefit of—others (1 Pet. 4:10).

5. As we develop and exercise our motivational gift, we are free to apply it in any areas of ministry that we choose. Our motivational gift answers the question: Why do I serve where I serve? Motivational gifts are the driving force behind all effective and fruitful ministry service.
6. Motivational gifts are given us that, through their diligent exercise, God may be praised (1 Pet. 4:11).

Now we are ready to begin examining the motivational gifts in greater detail and go through the discovery process. But first, allow me to make a few suggestions that will help you discern your motivational gift.

First, please read through the details of *all seven* motivational gifts before trying to discern your particular gift. Our natural tendency is to see new information through the lens of our own background rather than receiving it objectively. This tendency can distort our discovery process and lead us to a false conclusion as to what motivational gift we've been given. For example, if you've always been an extrovert and have a passionate (and often loud!) personality, you might read through the characteristics of the prophecy gift and immediately conclude that it describes you perfectly. That would be a mistake; it is vitally important that we don't confuse external personality traits with motivational gifting. Our gift is an *internal* working of God the Father.

Similarly, if you dread public speaking you might be inclined to immediately dismiss the teaching gift solely because of that fear. That, too, would be a mistake. God the Father may indeed have gifted you to teach and there may be other ways to exercise this gift than speaking before large groups of people. Try to keep an open mind as you read through the descriptions of all seven motivational gifts, and don't allow your personality or background to cause you to rule out any of the gifts before you've studied each one in greater detail.

Second, do not rule out a particular gift simply because you do not identify with all of the characteristics listed. We are all different, and the same motivational gift will frequently manifest itself in various ways in different people. The list of characteristics is meant as a guideline; you will most likely only personally match two out of every three of the characteristics listed.

Finally, as you read the descriptions of the seven motivational gifts, please remind yourself that you're looking primarily at an internal motivation as opposed to an external response. An introvert with the prophecy gift, for example, might initially be a person who loathes conflict. That shouldn't eliminate prophecy from consideration as the motivational gift. The question becomes how that person responds internally when seeing Christ's name dishonored or confronted with blatant sin. It is the internal affect that will lead to discovering this person's motivational gift.

Similarly, a person who has been trained as a leader, such as a military officer, might be very good at leading when viewed externally. That is not the relevant issue. The question is how this person responds internally when leading in a church ministry. Does he or she feel excited and full of energy? Or does the assignment drain them of life and energy? The key is what is happening on the inside, and you are the person best equipped to make that determination for yourself.

With those words of caution in mind, let us move ahead with a study of the seven gifts of God the Father—the motivational gifts.

Chapter Eight

The Motivational Gift of Prophecy

"If a man's gift is prophesying, let him use it in proportion to his faith."

Romans 12:6

Perhaps the most difficult motivational gift to understand from the New Testament perspective is prophecy. When we think of a prophet our minds usually turn first to someone who predicts the future. With regard to this aspect of prophecy, God has given clear instruction as to how His people can distinguish between a true prophet—one sent from God—with a false prophet. If a prophet entices his followers to worship other gods, he does not represent the one, true God, even if his proclamation is accompanied by miraculous signs and wonders (Deut. 13:1–5).

Similarly, a prophet who speaks words not consistent with God's words, or who makes predictions that do not come true, he likewise is not a prophet of God (Deut. 18:20–22).

Although we are all fascinated by this aspect of prophecy, found mostly in the Old Testament (though it occasionally appears in the New Testament), such predictions are not associated with the motivational gift of prophecy. At the risk of oversimplifying, it may be best to think of prophecy in three different ways: the office, the act and the gift. Though the three have several things in common, they also represent decidedly different areas of study.

The *office of prophet* was unique to the Old Covenant and provided direct representatives of God before His people. The list of Old Testament prophets includes, among others, Moses, Joel, Hosea, Isaiah, Jeremiah, Ezekiel, Haggai and Malachi. The last in this line of Old Testament prophets is the man who provides the link from the Old Testament to the New Testament: John the Baptist. According to the *New Bible Dictionary,* Second Edition, "The Old Testament prophetic line did not end with Malachi, but with John the Baptist, as our Lord expressly declares (Matt. 11:13)." The prophetic office throughout the history of God's people makes for an interesting study to be sure, but one can discover, develop and exercise the motivational gift of prophecy without a detailed understanding of the prophetic office.

The *act of prophecy* generally includes what is commonly referred to as a "prophetic utterance," words spoken by God's people under the guidance of the Holy Spirit. Some examples of the act of prophecy include Zechariah (John the Baptist's father) in Luke 1:67–79, Simeon in Luke 2:34–35, Agabus in Acts 11:28 and 21:10–11, and Paul in Acts 27:31–34. All of these are instances in which one of God's people was moved by the Holy Spirit to predict a future event, and in all of these cases that future event came to pass.

You may be thinking that the act of prophecy strongly resembles a manifestation gift of the Holy Spirit in that it is: a) inspired by the Spirit; b) distributed as He wills; and c) frequently a one-time event. If this thought occurred to you, you are absolutely correct. Unlike the other six motivational gifts, prophecy is also included in the list of manifestation gifts in 1 Corinthians 12:10. According to the New International Version text note for 1 Corinthians 12:10, the manifestation gift of prophecy is "a communication of the mind of God imparted to a believer by the Holy Spirit. It may be a prediction or an indication of the will of God in a given situation."

The examples noted above all represent the first kind of prophetic utterance; i.e., they are predictions. Examples of the second type of prophetic utterance, in which God's will is rightly discerned in a given situation, include Peter's sermon in Acts 4, the commissioning of Paul and Barnabas as missionaries in Acts 13:1–2, and Paul's rebuke of Elymas the sorcerer in Acts 13:8–11.

The most obvious demonstration of prophecy in this sense, however, is the New Testament itself. The writers of each New Testament book wrote under the direct inspiration of the Holy Spirit. I don't believe that many of these men had the motivational gift of prophecy, but all of them experienced the manifestation gift of prophecy. The books of the New Testament include both types of prophetic utterance.

Like the other manifestation gifts, the Holy Spirit is the source of prophetic utterance, and He distributes this gift in accordance with His will in order to accomplish His specific purpose. The act of prophecy, whether predicting the future or discerning God's will in a particular situation, differs from the motivational gift of prophecy.

If the motivational gift of prophecy differs from the office or act of prophecy, how then would we define this gift? According to John Calvin, in his commentary on Romans: "Hence, prophecy at this day in the Christian church is hardly anything else than the right understanding of the Scripture, and the particular faculty of explaining it, inasmuch as the ancient prophecies and all the oracles of God have been completed in Christ and His gospel."

The motivational gift of prophecy does not involve either predictions or new revelation, but rather the unique ability to bring a decidedly biblical perspective to bear in any circumstance. The person with the motivational gift of prophecy will develop an intimate understanding of the mind and heart of God, and seek to communicate this understanding to God's people in order that they might become more like Christ.

When prophecy is discussed from a New Testament perspective, it is often broken down into two categories of proclamation: "foretelling" and "forth-telling." We've already discussed foretelling—the predicting of a future event—and attributed it to the manifestation gift of prophecy. The concept of forth-telling describes the outworking of the motivational prophetic gift.

DEFINITION: The motivational gift of prophecy is God's enablement to understand His truth as revealed in His Word and to communicate this truth to others in a way that is both timely and relevant, resulting in the hearer's understanding, correction, repentance or edification.

Simply stated, prophets have an incredible heart for God and His Word. In their world, holiness is not optional. Surely, the prophet will continue to struggle with the sinful flesh, as we all do, but Christ's righteousness and obedience to His standard drives the prophet's ministry. There exists in the prophet an intense, internal desire for God's glory. A person with the motivational gift of prophecy will often experience a greater sense of passion for the kingdom of God than is common with the other gifts. This passion will often manifest itself externally, but even in the most introverted prophet a fire burns deep in the heart for the glory of the risen Christ. God's truth is received with a serious and sober mind, and it is often communicated with the same intensity as the Old Testament prophetic office.

CHARACTERISTICS

The motivational gift of prophecy is most evident in a believer when he or she is confronted with blatant sin. There is often an immediate, internal response of righteous anger, not because the prophet feels superior in any way, but because God's glory has been violated. It has been said that the prophet is jealous for God's glory, and this trait is most evident in the face of blatant disregard for God's Word. Even a prophet who by nature dislikes conflict will usually be moved to confront sin in a fellow believer. Unlike someone with the gift of encouragement, however, the prophet is more likely to bring correction by focusing on God's judgment than on His grace, urgently exhorting the offending party to immediate, heartfelt repentance.

The prophet often has a unique ability to speak a timely word of God's truth in a given situation. There is usually a strong and growing knowledge of God's Word, which always finds its way into conversations. The prophet doesn't read the Bible just as a matter of obedience or for academic reasons; the prophet mines each passage for the vital message that God has for His people.

As these truths are learned and internalized, the prophet is compelled to make them known. These words from Jeremiah perfectly describe what is frequently experienced by someone with this gift: "But if I say, 'I will not mention him or speak any more in his name,' his word is in my heart like a fire, a fire shut up in my bones. I am weary of holding it in; indeed, I cannot" (Jer. 20:9). This is a great example of the internal passion for God's Word and glory that usually accompanies the motivational gift of prophecy.

Just as the prophet rarely studies God's Word for purely academic reasons, he or she rarely shares God's Word for casual reasons; he or she expects a response. To the prophet, once God has spoken clearly through His Word, change should be inevitable in the heart and actions of the hearer.

For example, a pastor with the prophetic gift cannot end a sermon without a call to action. It is unimaginable to the prophet that someone can hear God's Word rightly proclaimed and not respond.

Similarly, when a layman with this gift must confront a brother or sister who is in sin, he or she expects and demands immediate repentance. Someone with the prophetic gift can understand no other response; when sin is exposed in the light of God's Word, how can anyone who names Christ as Savior not be moved to repentance? The prophet knows intimately that "the word of God is living and active. Sharper than any double-edged sword, it penetrates even to dividing soul and spirit, joints and marrow; it judges the thoughts and attitudes of the heart" (Heb. 4:12). So powerful a word demands an immediate response.

Other common characteristics of someone with the prophetic gift include that they are discerning, compelling, uncompromising, authoritative and convicting. The prophet who is by nature extroverted might also appear bold, outspoken and even confrontational. Remember that every prophet will not identify with every characteristic noted above. This gift is often easier to discern in someone who is outgoing and extroverted, but even someone who is quiet and shy by nature will feel these characteristics internally, though he or she may or may not demonstrate them externally.

THE GIFT OF PROPHECY IN JESUS

It is my strong conviction that Jesus, and He alone, perfectly displayed all seven of the motivational gifts. For that reason, as I describe each gift in this and the following chapters, I will give examples from Jesus' life where that particular gift was evident in His ministry.

Looking at how Jesus displayed each gift might help us to discern our own motivational gift. Please note, however, that we are now entering into the realm of my personal opinion. The Bible doesn't explicitly state that Jesus displayed all of the motivational gifts, nor do the passages I will cite as examples describe Jesus' behavior as being related to spiritual gifts. My purpose in using these passages in this way is simply to give us a better understanding of each motivational gift and its outward expression.

One example of Jesus demonstrating what looks like the motivational gift of prophecy is during His temptation in the wilderness (Matt. 4:1–11):

> [1]Then Jesus was led by the Spirit into the desert to be tempted by
> the devil. [2]After fasting forty days and forty nights, he was hungry.
> [3]The tempter came to him and said, "If you are the Son of God,
> tell these stones to become bread." [4]Jesus answered, "It is written:
> 'Man does not live on bread alone, but on every word that comes
> from the mouth of God.'" [5]Then the devil took him to the holy
> city and had him stand on the highest point of the temple. [6]"If you
> are the Son of God," he said, "throw yourself down. For it is written: 'He will command his angels concerning you, and they will
> lift you up in their hands, so that you will not strike your foot
> against a stone.'" [7]Jesus answered him, "It is also written: 'Do not

> put the Lord your God to the test.'" 8Again, the devil took him to
> a very high mountain and showed him all the kingdoms of the
> world and their splendor. 9"All this I will give you," he said, "if you
> will bow down and worship me." 10Jesus said to him, "Away from
> me, Satan! For it is written: 'Worship the Lord your God, and
> serve him only.'" 11Then the devil left him, and angels came and
> attended him.

Even in His severely weakened state, when Satan distorted God's Word in his effort to tempt Jesus, our Lord rebuked His enemy by rightly proclaiming the word of truth. It is interesting that, although Jesus was the one under attack, He seemed more concerned with the glory of His Father than with defending Himself.

A second example of Jesus responding in a way that seems to mirror the motivational gift of prophecy is during the cleansing of the temple (John 2:12–17):

> 12After this he went down to Capernaum with his mother and
> brothers and his disciples. There they stayed for a few days.
> 13When it was almost time for the Jewish Passover, Jesus went up
> to Jerusalem. 14In the temple courts he found men selling cattle,
> sheep and doves, and others sitting at tables exchanging money.
> 15So he made a whip out of cords, and drove all from the temple
> area, both sheep and cattle; he scattered the coins of the money
> changers and overturned their tables. 16To those who sold doves
> he said, "Get these out of here! How dare you turn my Father's
> house into a market!" 17His disciples remembered that it is writ-
> ten: "Zeal for your house will consume me."

Not only was Jesus confronted with blatant sin; this sin was taking place in His Father's house. Jesus responds as one who is jealous for God's glory. We see in our Lord a similar attitude in the pronouncing of God's judgment on Korazin, Bethsaida and Capernaum for their failure to repent

(Matt. 11:20–24), and as he rebukes the Pharisees for their hypocrisy and wickedness (Matt. 23:1–36).

Lest we begin to think the prophetic gift only operates in the negative context, i.e. exposing and confronting sin or declaring God's judgment, we need only look to Jesus teaching the crowds to see the positive side of this gift on display. Think of how Jesus taught the people in the Sermon on the Mount, how He made God's truth come alive in the parables, and how He sought to comfort His disciples after dinner on the night He was betrayed by Judas. The person with the motivational gift of prophecy will just as easily comfort the broken-hearted with God's truth as confront a person with their sin and call them to repentance.

The Gift of Prophecy in Others

I have found it an interesting exercise to try and discern the motivational gift of different people in the Bible. This is another area in which we are left to speculate since God's Word doesn't tell us which motivational gift any of His people possessed. Once we understand the seven gifts, however, and since we know that every believer possesses one, it is reasonable to think we can discern the gift of at least some of God's people. Once again, my purpose is not to make definitive statements about motivational gifts that can't be supported by the Scriptures, but simply to help us to identify with other believers who might have the same gift that we do. Many people I've taught have found this exercise very helpful in discovering their own motivational gift.

The first example I would cite as someone who had the motivational gift of prophecy is the apostle Paul. While I should note that some teachers see in Paul the gift of leadership, I am absolutely persuaded that his was the prophetic gift. Consider his response to his fellow Jews in Acts 13:

> [44]On the next Sabbath almost the whole city gathered to hear the word of the Lord. [45]When the Jews saw the crowds, they were filled with jealousy and talked abusively against what Paul was saying. [46]Then Paul and Barnabas answered them boldly: "We had

> to speak the word of God to you first. Since you reject it and do not consider yourselves worthy of eternal life, we now turn to the Gentiles. [47]For this is what the Lord has commanded us: "'I have made you a light for the Gentiles, that you may bring salvation to the ends of the earth.'"

I've always found it interesting that, though God made clear that Paul was to be the apostle to the Gentiles, whenever he entered a new city he generally went right to the Jewish synagogue. This pattern is (indirectly) explained in his epistle to the Romans, in which Paul's intense longing for his people, the Jews, to come to faith in Christ is clearly evident. Paul desired that the Jews would recognize their Messiah, and it grieved him deeply that the majority rejected Jesus' offer of salvation.

Despite this deep love for his people, however, Paul responded with a harsh rebuke when the Jews failed to respond to God's truth. The thought of God rejecting Israel and choosing a people from among the Gentiles was abhorrent to the Jews. Paul used strong language when he talked about confronting this issue in Galatians 2. He was passionate because the glory of God was at stake.

> [11]When Peter came to Antioch, I opposed him to his face, because he was clearly in the wrong. [12]Before certain men came from James, he used to eat with the Gentiles. But when they arrived, he began to draw back and separate himself from the Gentiles because he was afraid of those who belonged to the circumcision group. [13]The other Jews joined him in his hypocrisy, so that by their hypocrisy even Barnabas was led astray.

This is another example of the prophet in action. Peter was certainly among the most respected leaders in the early church, but when he dishonored Christ by separating from the Gentile Christians to preserve his reputation among the Jews, Paul was beside himself. Such hypocrisy could not be tolerated, and Paul publicly rebuked Peter "to his face."

Most of us would agree that a more ideal way to correct a brother or sister in Christ is to talk with them privately. That is generally good counsel, but at times the prophet will feel unable to exercise such restraint. When God's Word and His glory are at stake, strong passions are kindled within the Christian with the motivational gift of prophecy.

Another example of someone I believe had the motivational gift of prophecy is Jude, brother of James and half-brother of Jesus (Matt. 13:55; John 7:3–10; Acts 1:14; 1 Cor. 9:5; Jude 1). Consider the opening words of his one-chapter epistle, just after he greets the saints:

> [3]Dear friends, although I was very eager to write to you about the salvation we share, I felt I had to write and urge you to contend for the faith that was once for all entrusted to the saints. [4]For certain men whose condemnation was written about long ago have secretly slipped in among you. They are godless men, who change the grace of our God into a license for immorality and deny Jesus Christ our only Sovereign and Lord.

I noted that one of the primary characteristics of the prophet gifting is their response when confronted with blatant sin. They will experience a deep, internal response of righteous anger because God's glory has been violated. Jude had intended to write this letter about "the salvation we share," but was moved by the behavior and teaching of ungodly men to instead rebuke their lies and warn the saints. These false teachers that had secretly slipped in among the faithful were perverting the gospel of Jesus Christ, distorting the doctrine of salvation by God's grace through faith in Jesus Christ by attempting to change it into a license for immorality.

The Christian with the motivational gift of prophecy absolutely cannot abide false teaching. So great is their love for the Lord and commitment to His truth that a perversion of His Word is taken as a vicious, almost personal, attack. God's glory is at stake in the mind of the prophet, and a swift and unequivocal response is required when such false teaching is encountered. The prophet is moved to attack the lie, defend the truth, and protect the saints.

I suspect Jude was enthused about the idea of writing an epistle to encourage the saints about their common bond in Christ and to reinforce their understanding of the gospel of grace. However, when confronted with false teachers who had infiltrated the ranks of those to whom he was writing, his mood and purpose quickly changed: "I felt I had to write and urge you to contend for the faith that was once for all entrusted to the saints."

The mature prophet increasingly loves God and despises ungodliness. When he or she rebukes sin, it is done with passion and conviction. There is often a reminder of God's past judgment, accompanied by a warning against continuing in sin. The prophet's language conveys strong conviction and carries with it the expectation of an appropriate response. Note the strong and uncompromising language of Jude's rebuke:

> "They are godless men, who change the grace of our God into a license for immorality and deny Jesus Christ our only Sovereign and Lord." (v. 4)

> "Though you already know all this, I want to remind you that the Lord delivered his people out of Egypt, but later destroyed those who did not believe." (v. 5)

> "In a similar way, Sodom and Gomorrah and the surrounding towns gave themselves up to sexual immorality and perversion. They serve as an example of those who suffer the punishment of eternal fire." (v. 7)

> "Yet these men speak abusively against whatever they do not understand; and what things they do understand by instinct, like unreasoning animals—these are the very things that destroy them." (v. 10)

> "They are wild waves of the sea, foaming up their shame; wandering stars, for whom blackest darkness has been reserved forever." (v. 13)

> "These are the men who divide you, who follow mere natural instincts and do not have the Spirit." (v. 19)

Jude does not hesitate to declare these false teachers to be false Christians. Regardless of what they profess with their mouth, their actions make clear that they do not have the Holy Spirit and are not part of the body of Christ. Most of us are reluctant to ever make such a comment, one that appears to judge someone's heart and makes a definitive statement as to whether or not they are actually born again. Not so with the prophet, who remembers Jesus' teaching that "by their fruit you will recognize them" (Matt. 7:16, 20), and Paul's instruction that we are, indeed, to judge those inside the church (1 Cor. 5:12–13).

The prophet will never shy away from contending for the truth and rebuking those who would pervert the Word of God. To the prophet, one's faith in Christ is either confirmed or denied by his or her actions, and those whose lives contradict their verbal profession of faith will always be called to account.

THE "DARK SIDE" OF THE GIFT OF PROPHECY

Because we continue to live in the flesh, even our very best intentions are tainted with sin. As Christians, we are being conformed to the image of Jesus Christ (Rom. 8:29), and the process of sanctification is a work that God will be faithful to complete in us (Phil. 1:6).

That said, we will continue to struggle with the sinful flesh as long as we're on this side of eternity, either until our death or until Jesus returns for His church, whichever comes first. For that reason, in the flesh we are prone to abuse our motivational gift, allowing it to operate in us by the flesh rather than by the Spirit. For each motivational gift, therefore, I will include some caution signs that will help us determine when we've started to exercise our gift in the sinful flesh.

Because the prophet will have strong convictions about biblical truth, even in areas where there is disagreement among theologians, there can develop a fleshly tendency for the prophet to act as if they are always right. For example, if a prophet is persuaded that certain behaviors are required—or forbidden—on the Sabbath, he or she might start condemning fellow Christians who hold different views and fail to live up to their self-created standard.

Because they are passionate about God's Word, there can be a tendency to engage in a fierce disagreement when someone interprets the Scripture in a way they disagree with. The prophet can become overbearing and argumentative when not walking in the Spirit, thus negating any opportunity to positively impact those they seek to minister to.

The fleshly prophet can also become very condescending. Because they generally study and know God's Word to a greater extent than many Christians, they can become arrogant about their knowledge and lacking in humility. Likewise, when fellow Christians are struggling because of circumstances they may have brought upon themselves, the fleshly prophet may be more inclined to lecture and rebuke than to encourage and restore them. A prophet operating in the flesh can be stubborn, unwilling to receive instruction and unable to receive correction.

As passionate as prophets are for God's truth to reign in the lives of His people, and as jealous as they are for God's glory, when operating in the flesh they can quickly violate God's Word and dishonor Christ by acting in a supremely unloving way toward fellow Christians. This may have been the case with Paul in Acts 15:37–40, where he adamantly refused to allow Mark to take part in the second missionary journey. Mark had abandoned Paul and Barnabas on their first trip, so Paul refused to take him on the second. When Barnabas insisted they restore Mark, "they had such a sharp disagreement that they parted company" (v. 39). You'll learn more about Barnabas and his personality when we study the gift of encouragement, and I'm sure you'll conclude, as I have, that Paul's stubbornness was most likely the cause of the breakup of their partnership. This can easily happen when a prophet exercises his or her gift in the flesh.

It is helpful and wise for the person with the prophetic gift to ask a close friend to help him or her be accountable for the exercise of the gift. This friend should be given permission to immediately challenge them when the friend observes the gift being exercised in the flesh. Humility is a vitally important trait for the prophet if the gift of prophecy is to be used effectively, and accountability is a valuable tool in helping the prophet to consistently walk in the Spirit.

SUMMARIZING THE GIFT OF PROPHECY

The motivational gift of prophecy is a great blessing to Christ's church when it is exercised in the Spirit. The Christian with this gift will demonstrate an intense love for God's Word, which often encourages others to more consistent study. The prophet will insist on personal holiness so as not to dishonor God and will encourage others to uphold this same standard. When blatant sin is evident, the prophet will rightly confront the sin, reminding of God's judgment and exhorting to repentance. When there is hidden deception or a distortion of God's Word, the prophet will be quick to recognize it and bring the needed correction. The prophet is adept at bringing a timely word from God that leads to conviction, repentance or edification.

The prophet can earnestly and joyfully proclaim, along with the psalmist in the first Psalm:

> [1]Blessed is the man who does not walk in the counsel of the wicked or stand in the way of sinners or sit in the seat of mockers. [2]But his delight is in the law of the LORD, and on his law he meditates day and night. [3]He is like a tree planted by streams of water, which yields its fruit in season and whose leaf does not wither. Whatever he does prospers. [4]Not so the wicked! They are like chaff that the wind blows away. [5]Therefore the wicked will not stand in the judgment, nor sinners in the assembly of the righteous. [6]For the LORD watches over the way of the righteous, but the way of the wicked will perish.

Do you refuse to walk in the counsel of the wicked? Do you delight in the law of the Lord and enjoy meditating on His Word? Are you jealous for God's glory and willing to confront sin, both in yourself and in others? If so, it may be that you have the motivational gift of prophecy.

Chapter Nine

The Motivational Gift of Teaching

"If it is teaching, let him teach."

Romans 12:7

The motivational gift of teaching is a vital contributor to the health of the body of Christ. Jesus instructs in the Great Commission that we are to "go and make disciples of all nations" (Matt. 28:19). Note that He didn't say "go and make converts." Too often the evangelism ministry of the local church is focused on seeking to elicit a "decision for Christ" and then moving on to the next prospect. That is not what our Lord has called us to; we are to make disciples, seeking to lead His people into unity and maturity in the faith. Those with the motivational gift of teaching play an important role in this process.

Definition: The motivational gift of teaching is God's enablement to interpret, clearly explain and apply God's Word to everyday life in such a way as to instruct, nurture and train God's people, leading to increasing maturity and Christ-likeness in the life of the hearer.

Proverbs 2:6 states, "For the Lord gives wisdom, and from his mouth come knowledge and understanding." This truth is music to the ears of the teacher. The person with the motivational gift of teaching delights to read and study God's Word because it is the source of all knowledge and understanding. When having a conversation with a teacher, you will notice that God's Word will always be brought into the discussion. This is not done to impress or to feign spirituality; the teacher knows no other way to have a fruitful conversation. God's Word dwells richly in the teacher and it is always working its way to the surface. The teacher often has difficulty understanding those who are disinterested in learning God's Word.

In studying a passage of Scripture, whereas the prophet is focused on the *message* of the passage, the teacher is intent on finding its *meaning*. The prophet might be more inclined to communicate the *implication* of the passage while the teacher emphasizes the *application*. It would not be unusual for a teacher's thirty-minute daily devotional time to stretch into an hour or more without the person even realizing it. Those with the gift of teaching will become consumed with understanding the meaning of what they are reading and lose all track of time.

One of the teacher's most prized possessions is his or her study Bible. They cannot read through a passage without referring to the notes and cross-references, always pursuing a more complete understanding of what God is saying. If you have a friend with the teaching gift and don't know what to get them for their birthday, try *Strong's Exhaustive Concordance* or the *New Bible Dictionary*. He or she will surely become your friend for life!

CHARACTERISTICS

The teacher is able to communicate God's Word in such a way as to inspire others to greater obedience. Often an analytical approach is taken by the teacher, both in personal study and when teaching others. Also, the person with the motivational gift of teaching will insist on teaching the whole counsel of God's Word; it drives them crazy when single verses are pulled out of their context and taught with an incorrect meaning. When the worship leader invokes God's presence by stating "where two or three come together in my name, there am I with them" from Matthew 18:20, the teacher will cringe and mumble to himself, "That passage refers to church discipline, not to public worship."

When someone preaching the Gospel to non-Christians quotes Jesus as saying, "Here I am! I stand at the door and knock" from Revelation 3:20, the teacher will shift uncomfortably in her chair knowing that Jesus made this statement to believers, not to unbelievers. God's Word—taught in its entirety and in its proper context—is the passion of the teacher.

A pastor with the teaching gift is likely to be drawn to expository preaching and to teach through each book of the Bible verse-by-verse, whereas the pastor with the prophet gifting might be more inclined to preach topical sermons, highlighting the main message within a particular book or section of the Scriptures. The reason is that the teacher is conveying "head knowledge" and trusting that the Holy Spirit will guide it to the hearer's heart; the prophet seeks to preach directly to the heart. The teacher experiences great joy when explaining even the most obscure Old Testament passage, methodically unpacking it phrase by phrase and striving to make it understandable to the hearer.

The teacher has a unique way of making the complex simple. Though they can be very focused on intricate details in their own personal study, they are frequently able to break down complex biblical concepts and explain them in a way that is easily understandable to the layman. This gifting also lends itself to giving explicitly biblical counsel in all situations. The teacher spends a good bit of time in study, reflection and preparation, and this investment of time is clearly evident in counseling situations.

The person with the motivational gift of teaching is concerned with detail and accuracy. Even if this person is by nature disorganized and scattered, those traits, though they may be a hindrance, generally won't be as evident with regard to the study and teaching of God's Word. The motivational gifts are a supernatural endowment. As such, they will often lead to behaviors that seem quite contrary to who we are in the flesh. So it is in the life and ministry of the teacher.

Additional characteristics common to those with the motivational gift of teaching include that they are often disciplined (with regard to God's Word), perceptive, articulate, patient and diligent. Like the prophet, they are often perceived as speaking with authority. The teacher has an obvious reverence for God's Word, and by example leads others to a greater love for, and dependence upon, the Scriptures.

The Gift of Teaching in Jesus

One example of Jesus teaching in a way that is consistent with this motivational gift is in the fifth chapter of Matthew's gospel. Knowing that His hearers had some misconceptions about certain aspects of God's instruction, Jesus methodically clarified His Father's word with regard to various types of sin. He would begin with the statement, "You have heard that it was said," and then go on to explain God's truth in a way that was easily understood by His followers. Here are some examples:

> 21"You have heard that it was said to the people long ago, 'Do not murder, and anyone who murders will be subject to judgment.'
> 22But I tell you that anyone who is angry with his brother will be subject to judgment."

> 27"You have heard that it was said, 'Do not commit adultery.' 28But I tell you that anyone who looks at a woman lustfully has already committed adultery with her in his heart."

> 38"You have heard that it was said, 'Eye for eye, and tooth for
> tooth.' 39But I tell you, do not resist an evil person. If someone
> strikes you on the right cheek, turn to him the other also. 40And
> if someone wants to sue you and take your tunic, let him have
> your cloak as well. 41If someone forces you to go one mile, go with
> him two miles. 42Give to the one who asks you, and do not turn
> away from the one who wants to borrow from you." 43You have
> heard that it was said, 'Love your neighbor and hate your enemy.'
> 44But I tell you: Love your enemies and pray for those who perse-
> cute you, 45that you may be sons of your Father in heaven."

In this passage, Jesus deals with seven different misconceptions, patiently and authoritatively instructing His hearers in the truth of God's Word. His teaching was clear and easily understood.

A similar pattern emerges as Jesus privately instructs His disciples in Matthew 13. To summarize, Jesus had been teaching the crowds through a series of parables about the kingdom of God. One of these parables, frequently referred to as the parable of the weeds (Matt. 13:24–30), led Jesus' disciples to approach Him privately for a more detailed explanation.

> [36]Then he left the crowd and went into the house. His disciples
> came to him and said, "Explain to us the parable of the weeds in
> the field." [37]He answered, "The one who sowed the good seed is
> the Son of Man. [38]The field is the world, and the good seed stands
> for the sons of the kingdom. The weeds are the sons of the evil
> one, [39]and the enemy who sows them is the devil. The harvest is
> the end of the age, and the harvesters are angels. [40]As the weeds
> are pulled up and burned in the fire, so it will be at the end of the
> age. [41]The Son of Man will send out his angels, and they will weed
> out of his kingdom everything that causes sin and all who do evil.
> [42]They will throw them into the fiery furnace, where there will be
> weeping and gnashing of teeth. [43]Then the righteous will shine
> like the sun in the kingdom of their Father. He who has ears, let
> him hear.

If you read this section through to the end of the chapter, you'll see a beautiful picture of the teaching gift. We don't know why the disciples were struggling with this particular parable; of the four "kingdom" parables preceding this discussion they questioned Jesus only about this one. Once He had explained the meaning of the parable of the weeds, Jesus provided further instruction about the kingdom using three more parables and then asked His disciples, "Have you understood all these things?" (Matt. 13:51). Since they had come to Him for clarification, Jesus wanted to make sure He had explained Himself in a way they were able to understand.

Then Jesus concluded His lesson with a statement that reflects the heart of every teacher of God's Word: "Therefore every teacher of the law who has been instructed about the kingdom of heaven is like the owner of a house who brings out of his storeroom new treasures as well as old" (Matt. 13:52).

Those with the teaching gift derive the same joy from expounding the Old Covenant as they do the New Covenant, delighting to demonstrate the unity between the two and mining for the wealth of treasure in both.

The Gift of Teaching in Others

After Jesus, the most prominent example of the teaching gift in the New Testament is Luke, the author of both the third gospel and the book of Acts. Luke was a physician by profession (Col. 4:14) and a faithful companion of the apostle Paul (Philem. 24; 2 Tim. 4:11). Many passages in the book of Acts are written in the first person plural, indicating that Luke was actually traveling with Paul during some of his missionary work. The first passage that convinces me Luke had the motivational gift of teaching is in the opening verses of his gospel:

> [1]Many have undertaken to draw up an account of the things that
> have been fulfilled among us, [2]just as they were handed down to
> us by those who from the first were eyewitnesses and servants of
> the word. [3]Therefore, since I myself have carefully investigated
> everything from the beginning, it seemed good also to me to write
> an orderly account for you, most excellent Theophilus, [4]so that
> you may know the certainty of the things you have been taught
> (Luke 1:1–4).

Although "many" others had provided written accounts of the life and ministry of Jesus, Luke "carefully investigated everything from the beginning" in order to make sure that an accurate and trustworthy account was given. This attention to detail and insistence on accuracy is consistent with the motivational gift of teaching. Likewise, note the almost excessive detail given in chapter 3 of Luke's gospel:

> [1]In the fifteenth year of the reign of Tiberius Caesar—when Pontius Pilate was governor of Judea, Herod tetrarch of Galilee, his brother Philip tetrarch of Iturea and Traconitis, and Lysanias tetrarch of Abilene— [2]during the high priesthood of Annas and Caiaphas, the word of God came to John son of Zechariah in the desert.

Can there be any confusion for the reader as to the precise time period being described by the author? Think of a major event in U.S. history and how we might describe it. Many people remember exactly where they were and what they were doing when the first plane struck the twin towers on September 11, 2001. The same is true for President Kennedy's assassination, Neil Armstrong setting foot on the moon, or the end of World War II. How descriptive are we when referencing such important events? We simply refer to "9/11" or "Apollo 11" and expect everyone to know exactly what we mean.

In generations to come we might need to provide more detail in order to single out such an event, perhaps expanding a written description to "Neil Armstrong, the first person ever to set foot on the moon as part of the Apollo 11 mission in 1969." We would expect that even such a limited explanation should be more than sufficient for the reader to know what event we are describing.

Not so for Luke, whose description of this event might be expected to read something like this: On the 16th day of the seventh month in the year AD 1969—when Richard M. Nixon was President of the United States of America, Spiro T. Agnew the Vice-President and Thomas O. Paine the Administrator of NASA—during the year that *Sesame Street* debuted on National Educational Television (NET), which was the predecessor of Public Broadcasting System (PBS), and Mario Puzo's *The Godfather* became the best-selling book in America, the Apollo 11 spacecraft was launched from Kennedy Space Center Launch Complex 39A at 9:32 a.m. EDT, remaining in the earth's orbit for two hours and thirty-three minutes before..." You get the idea.

Coincidentally, another New Testament Christian who may have had the motivational gift of teaching is Apollos (no relation to the space program referenced above!), a Jew from the city of Alexandria. Consider the following from Acts 18:

> 24Meanwhile a Jew named Apollos, a native of Alexandria, came
> to Ephesus. He was a learned man, with a thorough knowledge
> of the Scriptures. 25He had been instructed in the way of the Lord,
> and he spoke with great fervor and taught about Jesus accurately,
> though he knew only the baptism of John. 26He began to speak
> boldly in the synagogue. When Priscilla and Aquila heard him,
> they invited him to their home and explained to him the way of
> God more adequately. 27When Apollos wanted to go to Achaia, the
> brothers encouraged him and wrote to the disciples there to wel-
> come him. On arriving, he was a great help to those who by grace
> had believed. 28For he vigorously refuted the Jews in public
> debate, proving from the Scriptures that Jesus was the Christ.

The fervor and accuracy with which Apollos taught, his "thorough knowledge of the Scriptures" and his vigorous defense of the Gospel all point to the motivational gift of teaching.

THE "DARK SIDE" OF THE GIFT OF TEACHING

Like the prophet, the teacher walking in the flesh can become puffed up by his or her Bible knowledge and act condescendingly toward those who don't spend as much time in God's Word as they do. They might also tend toward a constant, even arrogant, quoting of Scripture—not sharing verses to edify and build up another Christian, but rather intending to draw attention to the teacher's vast knowledge of the Bible.

Another habit the fleshly teacher might struggle with is the tendency to talk over the heads of the hearers. In teaching the Bible they might choose words that, though biblically accurate, are unfamiliar to the average Christian. Even in the most casual of settings the fleshly teacher might prefer "God's wrath demanded a blood sacrifice as propitiation for the violation of His decrees," to the easier-to-understand "Jesus' death on the cross paid our sin debt." A uniqueness of the teaching gift that we've already discussed is the teacher's ability to make the complex simple; the teacher exercising this gift in the flesh will often purposely do just the opposite.

There can also be a tendency for the fleshly teacher to become isolated and feed on God's Word purely for personal edification—and perhaps to impress others. This motivational gift, as all the others, is given for the building up of Christ's church. A teacher who is exercising this gift in the flesh can become content to study God's Word simply for the sake of studying, not for the sake of preparing to teach others. Conversely, the teacher who is walking in the Spirit will be compelled to share what he or she is learning to edify—not impress—others.

Still another area of struggle for the teacher who is exercising this gift in the flesh involves an uncaring attitude toward those being taught. Since the teacher is communicating to the hearers' mind (vs. their heart or emotions), the flesh can lead to being satisfied with simply having taught the truth, regardless of whether the hearers understood what had been said. There can be a sense of "that's their problem...I've done my part" when a teacher exercises this gift apart from the Spirit. While recognizing that changing a person's heart is ultimately the work of the Holy Spirit, the teacher walking in the Spirit still cares deeply about God's truth being internalized and impacting the life of the hearer. When a teacher fails to care about the effect of God's Word in the life of the hearer, it is certain that this gift is being exercised in the flesh.

Summarizing the Gift of Teaching

The motivational gift of teaching enables its possessor to interpret, explain and apply God's Word. The teacher has the unique ability to explain God's Word, even the most complex biblical concepts, in a way that is easily understood by the average Christian. The teacher gives special attention to accuracy and detail and often prepares to teach God's Word by devoting much time to personal study and reflection. Those with the teaching gift will study and teach the whole counsel of God's Word. They are often loving and helpful counselors, communicating biblical truth in a way that inspires greater obedience to the Scriptures.

The teacher often helps others develop a love for God's Word and a hunger and thirst for righteousness; not only do teachers enjoy doing so—they see it as their responsibility. They love to study the words of their Teacher and to joyfully impart those words to others, desiring that both they and their hearers will become more like Him.

> [39]He also told them this parable: "Can a blind man lead a blind man? Will they not both fall into a pit? [40]A student is not above his teacher, **but everyone who is fully trained will be like his teacher** (Luke 6:39–40 emphasis mine).

Do you love God's Word and delight in mining its riches? Do you enjoy increasing your own understanding so you can help others do the same? Is detail and accuracy important to you when God's Word is being studied or taught? Have you noticed a unique, God-given ability to make even the most complicated biblical concepts understandable to others? Are you eager to give biblical instruction and counsel, and do you desire to see others grow in their love for the Word of God? If so, it may be that you have the motivational gift of teaching.

CHAPTER TEN

The Motivational Gift of Encouragement

"If it is encouraging, let him encourage."

ROMANS 12:8

The Greek word *parakalon,* translated as "encouragement" in Romans 12, can also be translated "exhortation." I prefer the former term since the concept of exhortation in our current culture often carries with it a negative connotation that is not intended by the Greek word. People sometimes think of exhorting as "getting in someone's face" and urging them to accountability, whereas the notion of encouragement connotes empathy and comfort, a more accurate way of understanding this motivational gift.

> DEFINITION: The motivational gift of encouragement is God's enablement to present His truth in such a way as to strengthen, comfort and console others, guiding them willingly toward biblical behavior, urging them to positive action when needed and helping them grow in their love for God.

Like the prophet and the teacher, the encourager has a love for God's Word and for sharing it with others. The encourager is often a magnet for people who are hurting and in need of comfort. They love to talk about the promises of God. They are easy to talk to and convey a loving and caring attitude toward the person/people they are interacting with. When in the presence of someone with this gift you will feel genuinely cared for, sensing that they truly enjoy being with you. If you are hurting, you will often walk away from an encourager with a renewed sense of hope.

CHARACTERISTICS

The person with the motivational gift of encouragement is able to come alongside folks who are discouraged, offering words that bring comfort and consolation. The encourager has a profound trust in God and confidence in His promises. Some favorite passages of those with this gift might include:

> And we know that in all things God works for the good of those who love him, who have been called according to his purpose. (Rom. 8:28)

> For it is God who works in you to will and to act according to his good purpose. (Phil. 2:13)

> "For I know the plans I have for you," declares the LORD, "plans to prosper you and not to harm you, plans to give you hope and a future." (Jer. 29:11)

> I can do everything through him who gives me strength. (Phil. 4:13)

> And my God will meet all your needs according to his glorious riches in Christ Jesus. (Phil. 4:19)

> Delight yourself in the LORD and he will give you the desires of your heart. (Psa. 37:4)

> But seek first his kingdom and his righteousness, and all these things will be given to you as well. (Matt. 6:33)

> Until now you have not asked for anything in my name. Ask and you will receive, and your joy will be complete. (John 16:24)

The promises of God are particularly precious to the person with the motivational gift of encouragement, and these promises are frequently shared with those in need of comfort. Note, however, that the encourager blesses not only those who are hurting—even those in the best of moods will often find their spirits lifted after an encounter with an encourager.

The person with this gift often brings out the best in others. After spending time with an encourager, those lacking confidence will find themselves more confident; those who are discouraged will find encouragement; those who are exhausted will be refreshed; those wavering in their faith will be renewed; those finding it difficult to trust God will find themselves joyfully surrendering to His perfect will. Like the premier athlete who is able to elevate the performance level of his or her teammates, those with the gift of encouragement will help to strengthen the faith of those around them in the body of Christ. They motivate people to learn and to grow.

Whether an introvert or an extrovert by nature, the person with the gift of encouragement likes to be with God's people, especially one-on-one or in small groups. They will often be able to discern when someone needs to be ministered to and will take the initiative. Even in the midst of the most difficult trial, the encourager will often be the only one to see God working for the good. Encouragers *expect* to see God manifest His goodness and glory in all situations. Their confidence in God becomes contagious.

Those with this gift tend to be positive and affirming, supportive and reassuring. They are willing to confront sin when necessary but never in a superior or condescending way. The encourager rarely displays a "holier-than-thou" attitude; they are aware of their own sinfulness and have compassion toward those struggling with sin. They can challenge and motivate fellow Christians to want to be more like Jesus.

THE GIFT OF ENCOURAGEMENT IN JESUS

One example of Jesus demonstrating the gift of encouragement was in His encounter with a tax collector named Zacchaeus, recorded in chapter 19 of Luke's gospel:

> [1]Jesus entered Jericho and was passing through. [2]A man was there by the name of Zacchaeus; he was a chief tax collector and was wealthy. [3]He wanted to see who Jesus was, but being a short man he could not, because of the crowd. [4]So he ran ahead and climbed a sycamore-fig tree to see him, since Jesus was coming that way. [5]When Jesus reached the spot, he looked up and said to him, "Zacchaeus, come down immediately. I must stay at your house today." [6]So he came down at once and welcomed him gladly. [7]All the people saw this and began to mutter, "He has gone to be the guest of a 'sinner.'" [8]But Zacchaeus stood up and said to the Lord, "Look, Lord! Here and now I give half of my possessions to the poor, and if I have cheated anybody out of anything, I will pay back four times the amount." [9]Jesus said to him, "Today salvation has come to this house, because this man, too, is a son of Abraham. [10]For the Son of Man came to seek and to save what was lost."

You may not be aware of the social status of tax collectors in Jesus' day, but suffice it to say they were regarded as having slightly less integrity than robbers and prostitutes. Though Jewish, the tax collectors acted as agents for the Roman government. They became wealthy by defrauding their own people—extorting far more money than was required by Rome for taxes—in order to line their own pockets. Tax collectors were despised by their fellow Jews, and were under no disillusionment about their reputations.

How did Jesus treat this hated social outcast? He invited Himself to dine with him. Sharing a meal with someone in the culture of that day was a sign of respect and friendship. It is safe to assume Zacchaeus frequently dined alone; yet note how Jesus conveys honor and acceptance—in public, no less—by greeting him in a friendly manner and requesting the opportunity to visit his house and share a meal with him. Jesus was frequently criticized by the "religious elite" because of the company He kept; He demonstrated an obvious preference for spending time with "tax collectors and sinners" (Matt. 9:10; Luke 15:1).

I mentioned in the definition of this gift that the encourager will often guide people "willingly" toward biblical behavior. That is what happens to Zacchaeus. Jesus doesn't even mention his sin; there is no mention of the money Zacchaeus has stolen over the years or his need of repentance and restitution. Yet so encouraged is he by being in the Lord's presence and honored by having Jesus visit his home, Zacchaeus giddily announces that he will both give half his money to the poor and make restitution to those he has wronged. Suddenly faced with the very embodiment of truth and holiness, what had been of utmost importance to the tax collector—his money—was now simply a tool to be used for the glory of Zacchaeus' Savior.

Another example of Jesus as encourager is at the Last Supper. There is no way for us to comprehend what was going through Jesus' mind the night before He went to the cross. Not only would He suffer brutal physical torture and the most painful death imaginable, but for the first and only time He also would experience separation from God as He took upon Himself the burden of our sins. John's account of this evening begins with Jesus taking a towel and a basin of water and washing His disciples' feet (John 13). Then, even as He must prepare His disciples for what is to come, warning both of Judas' betrayal and Peter's denial, Jesus denies Himself in order to comfort His disciples in chapter 14:

> [1]Do not let your hearts be troubled. Trust in God; trust also in me.
> [2]In my Father's house are many rooms; if it were not so, I would
> have told you. I am going there to prepare a place for you. [3]And
> if I go and prepare a place for you, I will come back and take you
> to be with me that you also may be where I am.

> [26]But the Counselor, the Holy Spirit, whom the Father will send in my name, will teach you all things and will remind you of everything I have said to you. [27]Peace I leave with you; my peace I give you. I do not give to you as the world gives. Do not let your hearts be troubled and do not be afraid.

We get a glimpse of the personal torment and anguish Jesus experienced that night in Luke 22 as Jesus prayed alone in Gethsemane. Still, His main focus up until that time was trying to bring comfort and encouragement to His disciples. Those with the gift of encouragement will always put the needs of others ahead of their own, and Jesus was the perfect example of such selfless love.

THE GIFT OF ENCOURAGEMENT IN OTHERS

My favorite example of the motivational gift of encouragement in the New Testament is Barnabas, the apostle Paul's frequent traveling companion. Why do I believe Barnabas had this gift? The first clue is the nickname he was given by the apostles. Nicknames are usually descriptive of a person's physical or personality attributes. What do you envision when you hear the nicknames Slim, Stretch, Brain, Shorty, Weasel, Speedy, Motor-mouth or Hot-head? All of these nicknames would most likely give some insight as to the appearance or personality of the possessor. Do you know what nickname the apostles gave to Barnabas?

> [36]Joseph, a Levite from Cyprus, whom the apostles called Barnabas (which means Son of Encouragement), [37]sold a field he owned and brought the money and put it at the apostles' feet. (Acts 4:36–37)

We are so accustomed to hearing the name Barnabas that we forget it wasn't his real name. The fact that the apostles gave Joseph the nickname Barnabas, and that Luke made a point of noting that the name means "Son of Encouragement," is a clear indication that encouragement was a dominant and recognized trait.

The first time we see Barnabas manifest this motivational gift is in Acts chapter 9. The newly converted Saul of Tarsus (the apostle Paul), upon coming to Jerusalem to join with the leaders of the church, was rejected by the apostles, who could not believe his conversion was genuine. Saul had been personally responsible for the persecution of Christians and he was among the men most feared by followers of Jesus Christ. Note how Barnabas came to his aid:

> [26]When he [Saul/Paul] came to Jerusalem, he tried to join the disciples, but they were all afraid of him, not believing that he really was a disciple. [27]But Barnabas took him and brought him to the apostles. He told them how Saul on his journey had seen the Lord and that the Lord had spoken to him, and how in Damascus he had preached fearlessly in the name of Jesus. [28]So Saul stayed with them and moved about freely in Jerusalem, speaking boldly in the name of the Lord.

This brief description may not fully convey the desperation of Paul's circumstances. Because he had converted to Christianity, the Jews had conspired to kill him (Acts 9:23, 29). If he were to be similarly rejected by the Christian leadership, Paul would have had nowhere to turn. This was a pivotal moment in Paul's life and ministry, and Barnabas was there to help him. This relationship was continued several years later when the new church was planted at Antioch. Note the following from Acts chapter 11:

> [22]News of this reached the ears of the church at Jerusalem, and they sent Barnabas to Antioch. [23]When he arrived and saw the evidence of the grace of God, he was glad and encouraged them all to remain true to the Lord with all their hearts. [24]He was a good man, full of the Holy Spirit and faith, and a great number of people were brought to the Lord. [25]Then Barnabas went to Tarsus to look

> for Saul, [26]and when he found him, he brought him to Antioch. So for a whole year Barnabas and Saul met with the church and taught great numbers of people. The disciples were called Christians first at Antioch.

A number of years after their first encounter, when a pastor was needed to lead the church at Antioch, Barnabas personally made the journey to Tarsus in order to recruit Paul for this vital ministry. Up to that point in time, Barnabas may have been the only person in the worldwide church who encouraged Paul in his ministry. It would not be an exaggeration to suggest that Barnabas' encouragement played a critical role in the success and effectiveness of Paul's ministry, second only to the work of the Holy Spirit Himself.

Another example in the New Testament of one of God's people endowed with the motivational gift of encouragement was Silas, a leader in the church at Jerusalem (Acts 15:22). Not surprisingly, after Paul had a dispute with Barnabas that was so significant it resulted in the breakup of their missionary partnership, Paul chose another brother with the gift of encouragement to be his constant companion.

As an aside, those with the gift of prophecy do well to partner in ministry with someone with the gift of encouragement. This is true for a couple of reasons. First, because of the prophet's tendency to display righteous anger where blatant sin is involved, his or her message is often met with a defensive, emotional response, frequently leading to an argument rather than the repentance being sought. The more the person being rebuked resists and defends, the more insistent and passionate the prophet will become. In such cases it is very helpful to have an encourager present to act as mediator. The encourager's message is usually more readily received, and they can generally "soften the blow" by delivering the message with love and compassion. They can also help the prophet to see his own weaknesses with regard to communicating God's instruction.

Another reason the prophet-encourager partnership can flourish is that the prophet is frequently in need of encouragement. In a world where rampant sin and rebellion are the norm, the prophetic voice often falls on deaf ears. Even within the church, a person speaking out against sin, apathy and a lack of passionate commitment to Christ can often be perceived as an irrelevant extremist. The prophetic ministry is frequently in great need of the encouragement ministry.

Surely there were other reasons for Paul to take Silas on his second missionary journey, including his Roman citizenship (Acts 16:37) and the fact that he represented the leadership of the church at Jerusalem. Observing his ministry, however, leads quickly to the conclusion that Silas was an encourager. Consider the following from Acts 16:

> 16Once when we were going to the place of prayer, we were met
> by a slave girl who had a spirit by which she predicted the future.
> She earned a great deal of money for her owners by fortune-
> telling. 17This girl followed Paul and the rest of us, shouting,
> "These men are servants of the Most High God, who are telling
> you the way to be saved." 18She kept this up for many days. Finally
> Paul became so troubled that he turned around and said to the
> spirit, "In the name of Jesus Christ I command you to come out
> of her!" At that moment the spirit left her. 19When the owners of
> the slave girl realized that their hope of making money was gone,
> they seized Paul and Silas and dragged them into the marketplace
> to face the authorities. 20They brought them before the magistrates
> and said, "These men are Jews, and are throwing our city into an
> uproar 21by advocating customs unlawful for us Romans to accept
> or practice." 22The crowd joined in the attack against Paul and
> Silas, and the magistrates ordered them to be stripped and beaten.
> 23After they had been severely flogged, they were thrown into
> prison, and the jailer was commanded to guard them carefully.
> 24Upon receiving such orders, he put them in the inner cell and
> fastened their feet in the stocks. 25About midnight Paul and Silas
> were praying and singing hymns to God, and the other prisoners
> were listening to them.

Let me first state the obvious: Being beaten and thrown into prison was not unusual for the apostle Paul. During his years of ministry Paul endured every conceivable hardship (see 2 Cor. 11:23–27), eventually dying a martyr's death at the hands of Nero around AD 67. So what is unique about the particular beating and imprisonment described in Acts 16? It was what transpired "about midnight." Just for fun, try to identify which of these actions seems most out of place: stripped, beaten, flogged; thrown into prison, feet fastened in the stocks, singing hymns. It is interesting to note that of all the affliction and hardship endured by the apostle Paul during his life and ministry, this imprisonment with Silas represents the only recorded time he passed the painful hours away in song. People with the gift of encouragement raise the spirits of those around them, even during the most trying of times.

Perhaps more telling is Luke's description of what happened upon their release. We might expect these two men to be in dire need of some loving ministry once they returned to Lydia's house. Instead of focusing on their own needs, however, Luke records the opposite approach at the end of chapter 16 of Acts:

> 40After Paul and Silas came out of the prison, they went to Lydia's house, where they met with the brothers and encouraged them. Then they left.

One thing is certain: If I ever have to be stripped, beaten, flogged, jailed and chained, I sure hope I'm with someone like Silas.

The "Dark Side" of the Gift of Encouragement

It may be difficult to envision a negative side to the gift of encouragement, especially in view of the supportive and reassuring way people with this gift interact with those around them. Encouragement in the flesh, however, can turn quickly to superficial flattery. When the encourager fails to walk in the Spirit, he or she will simply appear as one who has attended too many "positive mental attitude" seminars. They will lack authenticity and depth in their personal interaction, defaulting to trying to make people feel good about themselves just so they will be thought well of. This dishonest application of the encouragement gift is a hindrance to spiritual growth, both in the encourager and the person being ministered to.

Interestingly, the fleshly encourager will often struggle with personal insecurity. Perhaps this is because they regularly see the impact their encouraging words have on others, and they long for such affirmation themselves. They can feel like they spend all of their time "feeding" others and become frustrated that no one seems to be meeting their own emotional needs. Since they are much more often a giver than a receiver of encouragement, they can begin to crave that which they so freely give away. This craving can lead to jealousy and bitterness—jealousy when they perceive someone else being affirmed, and bitterness when they feel unappreciated.

Although the encourager is well-equipped to confront someone struggling with sin—usually in a way that is gentle and compassionate—the carnal encourager will fail to confront sin no matter how blatant its appearance or how damaging its effects. When this happens, the encourager can actually appear affirming of the sinful behavior by becoming overly sympathetic. Such "encouraging" phrases as, "It's really not that bad," "we all struggle with some area of sin," and the ever-dangerous "don't be so hard on yourself" become an inadequate substitute for biblical counsel.

Insecure encouragers will become people-pleasers, doing or saying whatever is necessary in order to be affirmed and appreciated by others. They can develop an unhealthy need to be liked by everyone, often leading to shallow relationships in which confrontation is avoided at all costs.

Summarizing the Gift of Encouragement

The motivational gift of encouragement is among the most appreciated gifts in the body of Christ. Who doesn't need to be encouraged? Not only do we continue to struggle with our sin nature, we also often feel discouraged and defeated in our efforts to love God with heart, soul, mind and strength, and to love others as ourselves (Matt. 22:36–40). In the midst of such struggles we often find God's comfort and peace through the words of an encourager.

Christians with the gift of encouragement love the promises of God and delight to share them with others. They are uniquely gifted to come alongside their struggling brothers and sisters with comfort, consolation and godly counsel. They can gently guide God's people, joyfully and willingly, toward consistently biblical behavior. When fellow Christians have gone astray or backslidden, it is often the encourager who is most apt to bring them back to their church family. When brothers or sisters in Christ are grieving or suffering, the encourager comes quickly to their aid, recounting God's precious promises.

> [17]You hear, O Lord, the desire of the afflicted; you encourage them, and you listen to their cry, [18]defending the fatherless and the oppressed, in order that man, who is of the earth, may terrify no more. (Psa. 10:17–18)

Encouragers motivate healthy growth in other Christians and tend to bring out the best in those around them. They are trustworthy, supportive, reassuring, affirming, consoling, positive and motivating. They bring help and healing, kindness and comfort. Those who are wavering in their faith are encouraged and renewed; those strong and mature in their faith are motivated to even greater faithfulness and effectiveness in their ministry.

Do you love God's people and delight to encourage them? Are you deeply moved by God's promises, and do you find pleasure in sharing these promises with those around you? Are people often drawn to you, particularly those who are hurt or struggling? Do people seek you out for counsel, and do they receive your counsel with gratitude even when a gentle rebuke is needed? If so, it may be that you have the motivational gift of encouragement.

Chapter Eleven

Contrasting the Speaking Gifts

"If anyone speaks, he should do it as on speaking the very words of God."

1 Peter 4:11

Christians endowed with one of the three speaking gifts are often effective communicators of God's truth. Those with a speaking gift who pursue vocational ministry will often be drawn to the pastorate; similarly, gifted laymen will frequently serve as Sunday school teachers and small group leaders. Although communication styles will differ from prophet to teacher to encourager, on the surface these gifts can be perceived as being very similar. I've noticed in teaching on this subject that folks with one of these motivational gifts can usually identify immediately that they have one of the three speaking gifts, but there is occasionally some confusion as to which of the three they possess. For that reason, I thought it might be helpful to briefly contrast the practical outworking of the gifts of prophecy, teaching and encouragement.

The Speaking Gifts in Preaching and Teaching

Perhaps the most effective way to demonstrate the differences among the three speaking gifts is by looking at how each might be likely to communicate the same passage of Scripture. Let's consider the brief passage of Luke 8:22–25, commonly titled "Jesus Calms the Storm."

> [22]One day Jesus said to his disciples, "Let's go over to the other
> side of the lake." So they got into a boat and set out. [23]As they
> sailed, he fell asleep. A squall came down on the lake, so that the
> boat was being swamped, and they were in great danger. [24]The
> disciples went and woke him, saying, "Master, Master, we're going
> to drown!" He got up and rebuked the wind and the raging
> waters; the storm subsided, and all was calm. [25]"Where is your
> faith?" he asked his disciples. In fear and amazement they asked
> one another, "Who is this? He commands even the winds and the
> water, and they obey him."

THE PROPHET'S EMPHASIS

You may recall from our discussion in chapter 8 that the prophet is focused on the main *message* in any biblical passage. This contrasts with both the teacher, who is focused on the *meaning*, and the encourager, who is focused on the *promise*. This being the case, what verse(s) do you suppose the prophet will identify as the central text to use as the foundation for his sermon? My guess would be verse 25: "Where is your faith?" I also suspect that this question will be repeated numerous times throughout the course of the teaching.

At the risk of being overly dramatic, allow me to suggest the key points of this sermon in the hands of a capable prophet:

> "Do you find yourself frightened when the storms of this life threaten to overtake you? *Where is your faith?* Do you go running and looking for Jesus as if you have to wake him, as if He wasn't with you all along? *Where is your faith?* And after Jesus faithfully delivers you, do you find yourself asking, in utter disbelief that He actually came through for you, 'Who is this that was able to calm the storm?' *Where is your faith?*"

Cross references likely to be used in this sermon include Matthew 6:30: "If that is how God clothes the grass of the field, which is here today and tomorrow is thrown into the fire, will he not much more clothe you, O you of little faith?"; Luke 17:5: "The apostles said to the Lord, 'Increase our faith!'"; and Luke 18:8: "When the Son of Man comes, will he find faith on earth?"

If needed for emphasis, the prophet might add a brief exposition of 2 Corinthians 5:7: "We live by faith, not by sight," and close with Hebrews 11:6: "And without faith it is impossible to please God." Rather than seeing in this passage the comfort of Jesus' presence with us in the midst of our trials, the prophet might view it as a call to repentance for our debilitating lack of faith. With passion, emotion and, perhaps, a fist or two pounding on the pulpit, the prophet will lead us back to a renewed faith in an all-powerful Savior who is sovereign over all.

The Teacher's Emphasis

Needless to say, the teacher will have an entirely different take on this passage. Emphasizing neither the promises of God nor our lack of faith, the teacher will guide us into the boat, seating us next to the apostles as they huddled together, paralyzed with fear. The teacher will tell us which lake they were sailing on, how far out they went, what time of day it probably was when the storm hit, and why Jesus was so tired. Then he or she will describe typical weather patterns in that region at that time of year and explain why conditions were just right for such a squall, a storm so severe that it frightened even the most seasoned of fishermen.

The teacher will compare the parallel accounts of this passage in Matthew 8 and Mark 4, filling in some additional details in order to present a fuller picture of this event. You'll learn, for example, that the squall was "furious," that there was more than one boat, that it was evening and that Jesus slept on a cushion in the stern of the boat. If the sanctuary or classroom is equipped with power point, you will view a drawing of this kind of boat, along with a cross-section showing exactly where Jesus was sleeping.

After setting the scene with as much accuracy and detail as possible, the teacher will most likely move on to a verse-by-verse explanation of the passage. Whereas the prophet probably wouldn't be preoccupied with why they were in the boat, the teacher is compelled to share that their purpose was to "go over to the other side of the lake," for that is explicitly stated in verse 22. Since the text mentions the disciples getting into the boat, the teacher might point out where on the boat the entrance was located. She might also point out what was on the other side of the lake to give us an idea of why Jesus wanted to go there. Only when convinced that the hearers have thoroughly understood verse 22 will the teacher proceed to a similarly detailed description of what is taught in verse 23. And so on.

The Encourager's Emphasis

The encourager expounding this passage will most likely base the message on the second half of verse 24: "He got up and rebuked the wind and the raging waters; the storm subsided, and all was calm." There will be other points discussed, but the emphasis will be on the perfect calm that Jesus alone can bring to an anxious heart. Because the encourager can be sensitive to human needs, he might talk about the physical exhaustion that allowed Jesus to sleep in the midst of a violent storm, reminding us that when we are weary and burdened, Jesus knows exactly how we feel and He will give us rest.

The encourager might describe the storm, but not merely as an academic exercise. She wants the hearer to understand how the disciples felt that night, how very afraid they were and how their first instinct was to run to Jesus. We'll be comforted to know that this same Jesus, He who has power to rebuke the rushing wind and raging waters, continues to stand ready to meet us in the midst of our fear.

Rather than present Jesus' question, "Where is your faith?" purely as a rebuke, the encourager might also see it as a reminder of a great promise. It was Jesus, after all, who emphatically stated, "And surely I am with you always, to the very end of the age" (Matt. 28:20). The encourager might envision a caring and compassionate Jesus standing before those He has just saved, reminding them that their faith was rightly placed in Him. God promises never to leave or forsake us (Heb. 13:5). Where is our faith? It is in the one He sent to save us.

The encourager will likely also focus on the "fear and amazement" the disciples experienced, reminding us that a reverent awe is an appropriate way to see Jesus. The creation itself should inspire this response, as should the personal encounter every Christian has had with the risen Christ. How majestic our Lord, whose spoken word the wind and waves obey; who lays down His life only to take it up again because death has no hold over Him; our almighty and omnipotent Savior who loves us intimately, calling us His children, His brothers and sisters, and His friend.

The preacher with the motivational gift of encouragement cannot help but end this sermon—and every sermon—with a doxology, like the one found in Romans 11:

> 33Oh, the depth of the riches of the wisdom and knowledge of
> God! How unsearchable his judgments, and his paths beyond
> tracing out! 34"Who has known the mind of the Lord? Or who has
> been his counselor?" 35"Who has ever given to God, that God
> should repay him?" 36For from him and through him and to him
> are all things. To him be the glory forever! Amen.

The Contrasting Tendencies of the Speaking Gifts

Whether preaching, teaching or participating in a group discussion, a person with one of the speaking gifts will usually demonstrate certain tendencies with regard to his or her method of communication. I thought it might be helpful to summarize and contrast these different tendencies as follows:

Prophet	Teacher	Encourager
Speaks to heart	Speaks to head	Speaks to emotions
Focus on "destination"	Focus on "journey"	Focus on "delivery"
Lead to response/change	Lead to knowledge/growth	Lead to intimacy/joy
Emphasize the message	Emphasize the meaning	Emphasize the promise
Result: repentance	Result: understanding	Result: encouragement
Convey God's glory	Convey God's truth	Convey God's love

Keep in mind that these tendencies, as well as the sermon examples given above, are given as general guidelines only. Remember that the motivational gifts represent an *internal* working of God the Father; the outworking of these gifts can be as varied as the personalities of their possessors. An introvert who is given the motivational gift of prophecy, for example, may exercise this gift differently from an extroverted prophet.

When evaluating your own motivational gift in view of the tendencies cited above, or the characteristics listed in the previous chapters, please think first in terms of what you experience internally vs. how the gift is exercised externally.

SUMMARY

I hope in this chapter we've been able to resolve any lingering confusion for those who have determined they have a speaking gift but are not sure which one. One of the mistakes most frequently made in this assessment is to focus more on personality than internal motivation. If someone is outgoing and boisterous by nature, for example, folks will often automatically assume that person has the gift of prophecy.

If someone is by nature very detail-oriented, perhaps an accountant or engineer, folks may automatically assume they have the teaching gift. We must resist the temptation to judge by the externals, by someone's personality, vocation or education. The only way to help someone determine their motivational gift is to ask questions about what they are experiencing *inside*.

I should also note that just because someone is horrified by the thought of standing in front of a group and speaking, one of the speaking gifts cannot be ruled out. These gifts are an endowment of God the Father, and as such they can quickly overcome our own natural weaknesses. It is possible for someone formerly uncomfortable with speaking in public to begin to embrace it post-conversion (i.e. post-gifting), though this is not necessarily the norm.

On the other hand, you may have a speaking gift and never become comfortable or confident speaking to a large group of people. If so, I'm happy to report that public speaking is not the only way to exercise a speaking gift. Remember that we are called to "go and make disciples" (Matt. 28:19). Discipleship is largely a one-on-one endeavor, and the speaking gifts can be just as effectively employed in this setting as in preaching to the masses. My point is this: Don't judge whether you have a speaking gift simply by your desire/willingness to speak publicly to a group of people. Rather, judge by your internal desire to communicate God's Word to others and your effectiveness in doing so when the opportunity arises.

CHAPTER TWELVE

The Motivational Gift of Service

"If it is serving, let him serve."

ROMANS 12:7

Those with the motivational gift of service are the unsung heroes of the local church. Anonymous and frequently under-appreciated, the servants are the "engine" that drives the ministry of most churches. Not the high-profile ministries mind you. That would be far too conspicuous. The lower the profile, the better. Show-up at church for a 7 a.m. pancake breakfast and you'll often taste the handiwork of the servants. You might not see them, but you'll know they are there. Admire the flowers in the sanctuary for Sunday worship, or the nicely weeded flowerbed at the entrance to the church, or the newly wallpapered nursery, and you'll usually be admiring the serving gift in action.

DEFINITION: The motivational gift of service is God's enablement to joyfully perform practical and necessary ministry tasks that support and meet the needs of others.

The person with the motivational gift of service identifies with Matthew 20:28, where Jesus says, "the Son of Man did not come to be served, but to serve." Selfless, sacrificial service is what drives the person with this motivational gift. No task is too small, no ministry too unimportant, to attract the attention of the servant. Where there is a need, there the servant will be.

Characteristics

One of the unique attributes of people with the motivational gift of service is that they prefer to serve behind the scenes. If you want to upset them, just tell them the pastor is going to acknowledge them publicly for their service; they'll usually run and hide. Few people in the church do more ministry work—and few disdain attention more—than the servant. That is why they are often under-appreciated; most people are unaware of their immense contribution to the life and ministry of the church.

The servant loves to support others in ministry. There usually isn't one particular ministry that they enjoy. Their blessing comes simply from helping others in any way they can. One of their objectives is to make it easier for the leaders to lead. They will often insist on doing the jobs no one else wants. They'll pull weeds, scrub floors, buy groceries, set up tables and chairs, paint, bake, drive, visit…absolutely anything needed to further the ministries of the church. And always with a smile, no matter how tedious or repetitive the work may seem to others.

The servant actually senses God's purpose and pleasure in meeting the everyday, seemingly mundane responsibilities of ministry. They truly reflect Paul's counsel in Colossians chapter 3:

> 17 And whatever you do, whether in word or deed, do it all in the name of the Lord Jesus, giving thanks to God the Father through him.
>
> 23 Whatever you do, work at it with all your heart, as working for the Lord, not for men.

Those with the motivational gift of service attach immense spiritual value to practical service. Serving Christ through practical ministry is never a "have-to" but always a "get-to." For this reason, it is often difficult for a servant to immediately recognize his or her motivational gift. The teacher comes alive when teaching God's Word with accuracy and detail;

the prophet lives for those moments when God's message can be delivered with passion and power; the encourager is most at peace in the Lord when ministering words of comfort and reminding someone of the glorious promises of God.

As we'll soon see, the leader senses God's pleasure when leading His people; the giver is overwhelmed with joy at the opportunity to give God's money to God's work; the person with the mercy gift is most content when meeting the physical needs of one who is suffering. For each of the other six gifts, simply observing where they experience the greatest joy in ministry will point us toward their motivational gift. It is not nearly so uncomplicated with the servant.

Ask a servant what his absolute favorite ministry service has been and he won't be able to answer. He might wrinkle his brow, deep in thought, allowing his mind to run through all the various ministry opportunities he has absolutely loved. He might get frustrated at being asked to pick just one. Ask the servant which ministry she has served in that has provided the greatest sense of personal joy and fulfillment, and before realizing it she will have named every ministry in which she has served.

Observe the servant feeding the homeless—the love he shows to the recipients and the joy he displays while serving—and you'll be sure he must have the gift of mercy. Then watch a servant as she substitute teaches the six-year-olds' Sunday school class and you'll swear this is what God made her to do. When greeters are needed they'll joyfully greet; when the missions conference is being promoted they'll be handing out fliers; when the gymnasium needs to be set up for Vacation Bible School, there is the servant carrying tables and putting up posters. They experience such joy in everything they do for the Lord that it's almost impossible at first glance to identify their motivational gift. The servant does it all—and enjoys doing it all.

Other characteristics of the servant include being available, willing, helpful and reliable. If you ask a servant to meet you at church around 6:00 a.m. two weeks from this Saturday to help set up for a missions' breakfast, you won't need to call and remind him. In fact, he'll probably be there at 5:30 a.m., just to make sure the set-up team has freshly brewed coffee to greet them.

The servant will never think, *That's not my job.* If there is work to be done, the servant considers it his or her responsibility. They are dependable, faithful and ever alert to the needs of others, both individuals and ministries. The servant is humble and very loyal—loyal to the pastor, loyal to the elders and deacons, and loyal to ministry leaders. The person with the motivational gift of service is, above all, a selfless giver of self.

THE GIFT OF SERVICE IN JESUS

Much of Jesus' life and ministry revolved around serving others. His teaching emphasized this work and His actions modeled His words. Jesus made clear that greatness in His kingdom involves being a servant to others, and that His own mission was to serve rather than to be served. See Matthew 20:

> 25Jesus called them together and said, "You know that the rulers
> of the Gentiles lord it over them, and their high officials exercise
> authority over them. 26Not so with you. Instead, whoever wants
> to become great among you must be your servant, 27and whoever
> wants to be first must be your slave— 28just as the Son of Man did
> not come to be served, but to serve, and to give his life as a ran-
> som for many."

Having laid this foundation for His followers, Jesus emphasized the importance of our imitating Him by serving those in need. In Matthew 25, He reminds us that not only are we blessed as a result of our service, but also that serving others is the same as serving Him:

> 34"Then the King will say to those on his right, 'Come, you who are
> blessed by my Father; take your inheritance, the kingdom pre-
> pared for you since the creation of the world. 35For I was hungry
> and you gave me something to eat, I was thirsty and you gave me
> something to drink, I was a stranger and you invited me in, 36I

> needed clothes and you clothed me, I was sick and you looked after me, I was in prison and you came to visit me.' [37]"Then the righteous will answer him, 'Lord, when did we see you hungry and feed you, or thirsty and give you something to drink? [38]When did we see you a stranger and invite you in, or needing clothes and clothe you? [39]When did we see you sick or in prison and go to visit you?' [40]"The King will reply, 'I tell you the truth, whatever you did for one of the least of these brothers of mine, you did for me.'"

As noted above, the servant is able to identify and meet practical needs. This reflects the very heart of our Lord and His teaching. Do you see someone who is hungry or thirsty? Jesus teaches us to serve that person by providing food and drink. Do you know someone who is sick or in prison? Jesus encourages us to meet those needs by visiting them. Serve the stranger by inviting him into your home. Jesus' teaching on the importance of serving others emphasized first the meeting of practical, everyday needs.

As we've discussed, Jesus modeled what He taught. When Jesus was teaching and those who had gathered to listen were without food, Jesus met their need by feeding them (Mark 6:30–44; 8:1–10). When a bridegroom faced possible humiliation by running out of wine at his wedding banquet, Jesus intervened and provided wine (John 2:1–11). When Peter, a fisherman by trade and dependent on his daily catch to provide for his family, spent an entire night out at sea only to return empty-handed, Jesus joined him in the boat and guided him to a bounty of fish so large it began to break the nets (Luke 5:5–6).

Perhaps the clearest demonstration of Jesus' heart for serving occurred at the Last Supper, an account I alluded to in chapter 10. John's gospel (chapter 13) describes this incredible act of humility and service:

> [2]The evening meal was being served, and the devil had already prompted Judas Iscariot, son of Simon, to betray Jesus. [3]Jesus knew that the Father had put all things under his power, and that he had come from God and was returning to God; [4]so he got up

> from the meal, took off his outer clothing, and wrapped a towel around his waist. [5]After that, he poured water into a basin and began to wash his disciples' feet, drying them with the towel that was wrapped around him.

There was only one person in the room who understood what would transpire that fateful evening. One of His own would betray Him; Peter, the "rock," would deny Him; all the rest would abandon Him, fearing for their own lives. On this very night Jesus would begin a long and painful journey that was to end at the cross. Still, rather than focus on Himself, our Lord modeled selfless love and service by washing the feet of His disciples. Why? Because Jesus loved them: "Having loved his own who were in the world, he now showed them the full extent of his love" (John 13:1). Jesus chose to visibly display His love for the disciples, and at the same time He was setting an example for them. John continues:

> [12]When he had finished washing their feet, he put on his clothes and returned to his place. "Do you understand what I have done for you?" he asked them. [13]"You call me 'Teacher' and 'Lord,' and rightly so, for that is what I am. [14]Now that I, your Lord and Teacher, have washed your feet, you also should wash one another's feet. [15]I have set you an example that you should do as I have done for you. [16]I tell you the truth, no servant is greater than his master, nor is a messenger greater than the one who sent him. [17]Now that you know these things, you will be blessed if you do them."

Jesus taught, lived and modeled the life of a humble servant. His life is an inspiration to everyone with the motivational gift of service.

THE GIFT OF SERVICE IN OTHERS

One New Testament example of someone with the motivational gift of service is Epaphroditus, a believer from the church at Philippi who was sent to minister to Paul's needs during his imprisonment in Rome. Note the various types of service attributed to Epahroditus, as well as his selflessness, as recounted in the second chapter of Paul's epistle to the Philippians:

> [25]But I think it is necessary to send back to you Epaphroditus, my
> brother, fellow worker and fellow soldier, who is also your mes-
> senger, whom you sent to take care of my needs. [26]For he longs
> for all of you and is distressed because you heard he was ill.
> [27]Indeed he was ill, and almost died. But God had mercy on him,
> and not on him only but also on me, to spare me sorrow upon
> sorrow. [28]Therefore I am all the more eager to send him, so that
> when you see him again you may be glad and I may have less anx-
> iety. [29]Welcome him in the Lord with great joy, and honor men like
> him, [30]because he almost died for the work of Christ, risking his
> life to make up for the help you could not give me.

Paul's love and appreciation for his brother is evident. Pastors often have this kind of relationship with the servants in their flock. The church at Philippi was very dear to Paul, as he was to them. Paul personally planted this church (Acts 16:11–15) and they continued in partnership with him throughout his life and ministry (Phil. 1:5; 4:10, 15–16). When Paul was under house arrest in Rome and the church at Philippi wanted to provide aid and supplies, Epaphroditus was the eager and faithful servant chosen by the church to carry these gifts (Phil. 4:18).

Paul describes Epaphroditus as a "fellow worker and fellow soldier," indicating that he not only ministered to Paul's needs (Phil. 2:25) but also assisted Paul in his ministry to others. Epaphroditus was to be honored for his faithful service (v. 29) because he risked his own life in order to serve Paul (v. 30). And as is typical of the selfless nature of the Christian with the motivational gift of service, even in the midst of his own illness that brought him close to death (v. 27), Epaphroditus' focus was on his brothers and sisters back home: "For he longs for all of you and is distressed because you heard he was ill" (v. 26).

When we observe a fellow Christian serving in a variety of areas, much as Epahproditus did—visiting prisoners, bringing food and supplies, caring and encouraging, serving alongside the pastor, willing to endure long, difficult journeys in order to meet the needs of others—and doing so with a selflessness that mirrors Jesus' example, we can be confident that we are observing the motivational gift of service.

Another New Testament figure that demonstrated the gift of service is John Mark, author of one of the four gospels and occasional traveling companion of Paul, Barnabas and Peter. Although John Mark is mentioned only sporadically throughout the New Testament and none of the passages are very detailed, a look at these passages together gives us a well-rounded picture of his ministry service.

> When this had dawned on him, he went to the house of Mary the mother of John, also called Mark, where many people had gathered and were praying. (Acts 12:12)

> When Barnabas and Saul had finished their mission, they returned from Jerusalem, taking with them John, also called Mark. (Acts 12:25)

> When they arrived at Salamis, they proclaimed the word of God in the Jewish synagogues. John was with them as their helper. (Acts 13:5)

> Some time later Paul said to Barnabas, "Let us go back and visit the brothers in all the towns where we preached the word of the Lord and see how they are doing." Barnabas wanted to take John, also called Mark, with them, but Paul did not think it wise to take him, because he had deserted them in Pamphylia and had not continued with them in the work. They had such a sharp disagreement that they parted company. Barnabas took Mark and sailed for Cyprus, but Paul chose Silas and left, commended by

> the brothers to the grace of the Lord. He went through Syria and Cilicia, strengthening the churches. (Acts 15:36–39)

> My fellow prisoner Aristarchus sends you his greetings, as does Mark, the cousin of Barnabas. (You have received instructions about him; if he comes to you, welcome him.) (Col. 4:10)

> Epaphras, my fellow prisoner in Christ Jesus, sends you greetings. And so do Mark, Aristarchus, Demas and Luke, my fellow workers. (Philem. 23–24)

> Only Luke is with me. Get Mark and bring him with you, because he is helpful to me in my ministry. (2 Tim. 4:11)

One of the things John Mark is most noted for is causing the breakup of the Paul/Barnabas missionary team. You'll note in the Acts 15 passage (above) that John Mark had accompanied them on their first missionary journey, only to abandon Paul and Barnabas in Pamphylia and return home to Jerusalem. We aren't given much detail regarding the circumstances surrounding John Mark's desertion, but obviously Paul was not impressed with his reasons, whatever they were. Paul and Barnabas had been, to that point, virtually inseparable. At least in terms of the expectation of those he was serving with, it wouldn't be inaccurate to suggest that John Mark failed in his service to Paul and the spread of the Gospel.

So what makes me think John Mark had the motivational gift of service? One reason is that, despite the fact that he wasn't cut out for missionary work, when the team was assembled again for the second missionary journey, there was John Mark volunteering to serve. It didn't seem to matter that he'd had a bad experience; what mattered is that there was a need. Even when faced with Paul's criticism and refusal to take him, John Mark persevered in his desire to support this ministry. Whether Barnabas defended John Mark because he was his cousin (Col. 4:10) or, as I strongly believe, because Barnabas had the motivational gift of encouragement,

John Mark was willing to once again endure the hardship of foreign missions in order to serve others.

It is clear also that John Mark eventually won his way back into Paul's favor as a result of his committed and consistent service in the church. Note some of the observations and comments made about John Mark throughout the New Testament: His home was used for a prayer gathering in Jerusalem (Acts 12:12); he accompanied Paul and Barnabas on their inaugural missions trip (Acts 12:25) as their "helper" (Acts 13:5); he accompanied Barnabas on his second missionary journey (Acts 15:39); he later returned to Paul's service during his imprisonment (Col. 4:10) and was among a small group referred to as Paul's "fellow workers" (Philem. 24); his presence was requested by Paul at the end of his life, when everyone else—save for Luke—had deserted him (2 Tim. 4:11).

As with Epahroditus, in John Mark we see a commitment to serve, always in a supporting role, and a willingness to do whatever is needed to further the cause of Christ. He was willing to endure personal hardship and inconvenience for the sake of assisting those in ministry. John Mark was viewed as a faithful "helper," and to this day Christians around the world continue to benefit from one of his last acts of service to Christ's church: the gospel of Mark.

THE "DARK SIDE" OF THE GIFT OF SERVICE

There may be a significant difference between the gift of service operating in the flesh vs. the dark side of the other motivational gifts. Since the servant is by nature others-focused, and generally tends to consider others as more important than self (Phil. 2:3), the damage done by serving in the flesh tends to be more internal than external. That is to say, when this motivational gift is operating in the flesh, it is usually the servant who suffers most because the dark side of this gift rarely works its way to the outside.

One effect of the flesh on the gift of service is a tendency toward being judgmental. The servant tries to be "all things to all people." No task is too small or insignificant to get the servant's attention. For that reason, the servant can begin to experience a condescending frustration with fellow Christians who aren't nearly as willing to take on the menial tasks. A servant operating in the flesh will spend many a Sunday morning worship service looking down on members of the congregation as various church leaders plead for help in unfilled positions in their ministries. Since the servant is willing to serve whenever and wherever there is a need, in the flesh they can be quick to judge those less willing and to look down on those serving in fewer ministry areas.

This tendency in the carnal servant can quickly lead to the second fleshly trait: bitterness. One might argue that, at least at times, the servant is entitled to be frustrated with the perceived apathy of most church members. After all, if everyone would willingly serve, no one person would bear such a large burden that burnout becomes inevitable. But I'm referring here to actual bitterness, a cancerous internal emotion that eats away at the servant's heart. What used to be joyful service will become tedious obligation. The smile will be gone, replaced by a subtle but continual mumbling under one's breath, pointing the finger at the many unfaithful saints who care only about themselves. If this bitterness is not nipped in the bud, it will eventually rob the servant of the joy in exercising the gift and, in time, begin to negatively impact relationships within the church.

As you might expect, another characteristic of a servant operating in the flesh is pride. Makes sense, doesn't it? Surely anyone who is serving in a dozen different ministries will be given to feelings of pride in a moment of weakness. When you think about it, there are probably only two fleshly responses for the faithful servant when faced with the many "pew-sitters" who refuse to involve themselves in the ministry of the local church: bitterness or pride. The former serves with a hardening heart, angry that they have to do everything while others enjoy the fruit of their labor. The latter serves with a sense of "no one can outperform me." If another member of the church is honored publicly for their faithful service, the carnal servant's private thoughts might include, *Big deal—I serve in twice as many ministries, and you don't see me craving attention like that!*

Not having the motivational gift of service myself I can only speculate on this matter, but I suspect that the servant is less apt to operate in the flesh than those with the other six gifts. Servants simply love to serve. But once the flesh takes over, condescension, frustration, bitterness, pride, and the tendency to judge others is not far behind.

SUMMARIZING THE GIFT OF SERVICE

The motivational gift of service, when operating in the Spirit, is a wonderful thing to behold. The servant is divinely gifted to identify the practical tasks that need to be accomplished in any ministry, and to joyfully undertake those tasks and see them through to completion. The servant prefers to keep a low profile as a tireless worker who seeks to avoid recognition. This gifting experiences its greatest joy when ministry leaders are freed up to cast vision and advance the cause of Christ because faithful servants are performing the difficult work of ministry. The servant serves so the leaders can lead.

The gift of service can be difficult to identify at first glance because the servant enjoys most every area of ministry. This motivational gift can easily be confused with the gifts of encouragement, teaching, giving and mercy because the servant is willing to serve—and usually serves very effectively—in any capacity. The servant senses God's pleasure when performing even the most mundane of tasks. They are most fulfilled when helping others and attach spiritual value to practical acts of service. The person with the motivational gift of service can become almost overwhelmed with joy when contemplating the privilege of serving the Lord, feeling those same emotions felt by Jesus' mother at the thought of bearing the long-awaited Messiah:

> "My soul glorifies the Lord and my spirit rejoices in God my Savior, for he has been mindful of the humble state of his servant." (Luke 1:46–48)

The servant counts it an immense honor to serve Christ, doing "all in the name of the Lord Jesus, giving thanks to God the Father through him"

(Col. 3:17). The servant is available and willing, helpful and reliable, loyal and dependable. Those with the motivational gift of service are always alert to the needs of others and they work with selfless abandon to meet those needs.

Have you never met a ministry opportunity you didn't immediately embrace? Do you find it difficult to name your favorite ministry experience because you've so enjoyed everything you've been involved in? Do you willingly sacrifice convenience, time and personal comfort for the sake of assisting others in ministry? Do you find yourself smiling incessantly when serving, regardless of the type of work, because it is such an incredible blessing to be a part of what God is doing in the world? If so, it may be that you have the motivational gift of service.

Chapter Thirteen

The Motivational Gift of Giving

"If it is contributing to the needs of others, let him give generously."

Romans 12:8

Few in vocational ministry would dispute the vital necessity of the motivational gift of giving. Countless are the new ministry ventures in every generation funded largely by those with this gift: the building of new churches and Christian schools, the ongoing support of both local and foreign missionaries, the implementation of vision cast by pastors, the feeding of poor and hungry around the world. A significant portion of the work of advancing the Gospel is funded through the exercise of the motivational gift of giving. Surely we all participate in giving to kingdom causes, but few to the level of those with this gift.

> Definition: The motivational gift of giving is God's enablement to liberally contribute money and material resources to the work of the Lord with a joyful, cheerful heart.

Although the generous giver is much appreciated by church leaders and vocational ministers, no one appreciates their ability to give more than they do themselves. Being able to contribute to the Lord's work brings them joy beyond measure. Those with the gift of giving are frequently moved to proclaim with King David: "But who am I, and who are my people, that we should be able to give as generously as this? Everything comes from you, and we have given you only what comes from your hand." (1 Chron. 29:14)

Indeed, people with this motivational gift see the act of giving very differently from most Christians. They not only rejoice in God's provision of the resources to give, they also are humbled by the fact that God allows them to participate in funding His work. Whereas most Christians give regularly, even generously, to the Lord's work, the majority does so simply as a matter of obedience. To be sure, we all derive some level of joy from our giving; any time we give to the Lord, it is a demonstration of faith, which should result in great blessing. But most Christians never experience the same overwhelming sense of joy when contributing financial resources to the Lord's work—the deep level of satisfaction and fulfillment—as is enjoyed by those with the gift of giving.

CHARACTERISTICS

One common—and very notable—characteristic of folks with the motivational gift of giving is that they tend to manage their finances very well. Good money management often comes naturally to the generous giver. Their diligence in this area is borne out of necessity: the better their cash management, the more resources they'll have available for giving to God's work.

One of the biblical truths about money is that those who manage it wisely will be entrusted with more (Matt. 25:14–30). Never is this more evident than with the generous giver. He doesn't see his own needs as the reason to accumulate wealth; his concern is seeing the Great Commission fulfilled during his lifetime. Excess financial resources are simply a means of accelerating the spread of the Gospel and caring for those in need, not a license to "build bigger barns," as the rich fool did in Jesus' parable (see Luke 12:16–21).

The giver will often make a decision to limit her lifestyle in order to maximize the ability to give more away. Those blessed by God with above-average material wealth would downsize their lifestyle in a heartbeat should it be necessary in order to continue giving generously. Wealthy givers are never controlled by their material possessions, and they generally see everything they have as being available for ministry to others.

Generous givers love visionary leaders. Even though they delight immensely in being regular supporters of ongoing ministry, givers very much enjoy being involved in funding new methods of advancing the cause of Christ. Their enthusiasm for funding new ministry ventures is often contagious, frequently making the work of fundraising much easier for ministry leaders. In fact, many with this gift find great satisfaction in cultivating an increased heart for giving in those around them.

Folks with the motivational gift of giving have an innate ability to trust God for His provision. They understand that God owns everything, and they never doubt His ability to provide for their needs. As a result, the generous giver is much more likely to give sacrificially than the typical Christian. An unwavering ability to trust God is a common trait among those with this gift.

Many people with the gift of giving have an ability to create wealth. For some it would seem that every business venture is successful, as if they attract money without even trying. This is not to suggest that everyone with the gift of giving has accumulated a lot of material wealth from which to give. Whether rich or poor in the eyes of the world, the generous giver tends to be an excellent manager of whatever amount of resources God has entrusted to him.

Another admirable quality associated with those possessing this motivational gift is that their giving is never done with any thought of receiving. Many gifts, if we are honest with ourselves, are given with at least partially selfish motives. Whether in pursuit of God's material blessing or attention from other Christians, many kingdom gifts are given with less than pure intentions. Not so with the giver who is exercising his gift in the Spirit. He prefers making gifts that are given anonymously, desiring to avoid personal attention, and to make sure that God receives the glory for the gift.

The person with the motivational gift of giving takes very seriously God's call to faithful stewardship. The Bible makes clear that God owns everything and we are stewards—or managers—of His resources. Few take this responsibility more seriously than the giver. They understand their accountability to God for every penny that runs through their fingertips, and they never take lightly their position as manager of God's money. It is His glory they seek when making financial decisions.

The giver is responsible, resourceful and very charitably inclined. They are generally content regardless of their economic position and grateful for all that God has given them, be it little or plenty. The giver is more than willing to do without in order that someone else might be filled. They are usually disciplined with regard to money and often enjoy teaching biblical financial principles to others in order to encourage them in their stewardship of God's resources.

THE GIFT OF GIVING IN JESUS

Nowhere in the Scriptures do we find a more giving person than Jesus Christ. We've noted that three common characteristics of those with the motivational gift of giving are: their heart for giving financial resources to kingdom work, their ability to trust God to provide for all of their needs, and the desire to teach others how to be faithful stewards. All of these qualities are evident in the life and ministry of Jesus.

Jesus freely gave and frequently taught about giving. He gave rest to the weary (Matt. 11:28), sight to the blind (Matt. 9:27–30), food to the hungry (John 6:1–13) and His life for our salvation (Matt. 20:28). He encouraged His followers to give to the needy (Matt. 6:3), to give freely (Matt. 10:8) and to everyone who asks (Luke 6:30), and to be willing to give all we have in order to be identified as His disciples (Luke 14:33).

Jesus demonstrated His heart for giving—and for trusting in His Father's provision—in the Sermon on the Mount. In the opening verses (Matt. 6:1–4), He taught us how to give; i.e., that we should not seek to draw attention to ourselves but should rather do our giving "in secret." In verses 19–21, He encourages us that by giving we store up treasure in heaven. He concludes these thoughts (vv. 25–34) by reminding us that we need not worry about money and material possessions; our loving Father knows what we need and will never fail to provide. Our natural tendency is to fret about giving because we're concerned about meeting our own needs. Jesus taught that it is far more blessed to give than to receive (Acts 20:35) and that we can give generously with absolute assurance that our own needs will be met by our loving Father.

As for Jesus' interest in promoting biblical stewardship, most of the church's understanding of this topic comes from Jesus' teaching. The main tenet of biblical stewardship is the fact that God owns everything, and it is He alone who is able to provide for all of our needs. This truth is brought out in Matthew 6:25-34 (see above), and God's ownership is also depicted in Jesus' classic teaching on this topic, the parable of the talents, in Matthew 25:

> 14"Again, it will be like a man going on a journey, who called his servants and entrusted his property to them. 15To one he gave five talents of money, to another two talents, and to another one talent, each according to his ability. Then he went on his journey. 16The man who had received the five talents went at once and put his money to work and gained five more. 17So also, the one with the two talents gained two more. 18But the man who had received the one talent went off, dug a hole in the ground and hid his master's money. 19After a long time the master of those servants returned and settled accounts with them. 20The man who had received the five talents brought the other five. 'Master,' he said, 'you entrusted me with five talents. See, I have gained five more.' 21His master replied, 'Well done, good and faithful servant! You have been faithful with a few things; I will put you in charge of many things. Come and share your master's happiness!' 22The man with the two talents also came. 'Master,' he said, 'you entrusted me with two talents; see, I have gained two more.' 23His master replied, 'Well done, good and faithful servant! You have been faithful with a few things; I will put you in charge of many things. Come and share your master's happiness!' 24Then the man who

> had received the one talent came. 'Master,' he said, 'I knew that you are a hard man, harvesting where you have not sown and gathering where you have not scattered seed. 25So I was afraid and went out and hid your talent in the ground. See, here is what belongs to you.' 26His master replied, 'You wicked, lazy servant! So you knew that I harvest where I have not sown and gather where I have not scattered seed? 27Well then, you should have put my money on deposit with the bankers, so that when I returned I would have received it back with interest. 28'Take the talent from him and give it to the one who has the ten talents. 29For everyone who has will be given more, and he will have an abundance. Whoever does not have, even what he has will be taken from him. 30And throw that worthless servant outside, into the darkness, where there will be weeping and gnashing of teeth.'"

In addition to the fact that God (here referred to as the Master) owns everything, another important fact of biblical stewardship is that He alone determines how much money each of us is to be entrusted with. This truth is conveyed in verses 14–15, as is the fact that this allocation of resources is based on our "ability" to manage them properly.

A third stewardship principle taught by Jesus is that when we fail to manage God's money wisely, we risk having those resources taken away from us (v. 28).

A fourth important principle is that those who manage God's resources in accordance with His instruction will be entrusted with even greater responsibility (v. 29). Suffice it to say that everything the generous giver knows—or needs to know—about faithful stewardship he or she has learned from Jesus.

The Gift of Giving in Others

One of the more prominent New Testament figures that most likely possessed the motivational gift of giving is Matthew, the tax-collector-turned-apostle and author of the first gospel. The well-known extortionate practices of tax collectors most likely made the pre-conversion Matthew a wealthy man. It would appear from Luke 5:29 that Matthew (also called Levi) owned a large home, at which he held a "great banquet" for Jesus and entertained a "large crowd of tax collectors and others." Tax collectors were able to extort almost unlimited "taxes" from their fellow Jews, frequently resulting in a significant accumulation of personal wealth.

When Luke tells us that "Levi got up, left everything and followed him" (Luke 5:28), we might reasonably assume that Matthew left more behind than the others. Perhaps this willingness to walk away from his wealth in order to follow Jesus was a precursor to the motivational gift he would later be given.

Most of Jesus' teaching on giving, money and stewardship is recorded in Matthew's gospel. This is one reason I believe he had the gift of giving. Think of all the time the apostles spent with Jesus during His three-plus years of ministry, how much they saw and heard, how many lives Jesus had touched. When the time came for the gospel writers to record these events, each writer had to decide which words and events to include in his gospel. John makes this clear when he concludes his own gospel with these words: "Jesus did many other things as well. If every one of them were written down, I suppose that even the whole world would not have room for the books that would be written" (John 21:25).

Matthew devoted more of his gospel to financial issues than Mark, Luke or John. Some of the financial topics addressed by Matthew include: giving to the needy (6:2), storing up treasure in heaven (6:20), we cannot serve both God and money (6:24), God's provision of our daily needs (6:33), the rich young ruler (19:16–22), paying taxes (22:15–22) and the parable of the talents (25:14–30). With his typical attention to financial detail, Matthew was the only gospel writer who recorded the actual price paid to Judas for his betrayal of Jesus: "So they counted out for him thirty silver coins" (26:15).

The composition of Matthew's gospel—his emphasis on Jesus' teaching on giving, trusting God and biblical stewardship—convinces me that he possessed the motivational gift of giving.

Another New Testament figure who likely possessed the motivational gift of giving was Titus. In the eighth and ninth chapters of Paul's second epistle to the church at Corinth, we learn that Titus was involved in organizing a charitable campaign there in order to provide relief for the famine-stricken believers in Jerusalem (2 Cor. 8:6; see also Acts 11:28 and 1 Cor. 16:1–4). Any servant of Christ who is so inclined can be involved in organizing a giving campaign among God's people, but those with the gift of giving will usually have a broader impact than simply raising money—they will actually cultivate a heart of generosity and motivated giving among their peers. Note the impact that Titus had upon the saints in Corinth in terms of their desire to give:

> So we urged Titus, since he had earlier made a beginning, to bring also to completion this act of grace on your part. (2 Cor. 8:6)

> Last year you were the first not only to give, but also to have the desire to do so. Now finish the work, so that your eager willingness to do it may be matched by your completion of it, according to your means. (2 Cor. 8:10–11)

> I thank God, who put into the heart of Titus the same concern I have for you. For Titus not only welcomed our appeal, but he is coming to you with much enthusiasm and on his own initiative. (2 Cor. 8:16–17)

> For I know your eagerness to help, and I have been boasting about it to the Macedonians, telling them that since last year you in Achaia were ready to give; and your enthusiasm has stirred most of them to action. (2 Cor. 9:2)

> So I thought it necessary to urge the brothers to visit you in advance and finish the arrangements for the generous gift you had promised. (2 Cor. 9:5)

Several observations lead to my conclusion that Titus was blessed with the motivational gift of giving. Notice how, when Paul encouraged the church at Corinth to take part in the giving campaign for the saints in Jerusalem, Titus is the one he chose to organize the process (2 Cor. 8:6; see also 1 Cor. 16:1).

After a successful beginning to this campaign and the subsequent stalling, Titus enthusiastically took the initiative to return and encourage the church to complete the process (2 Cor. 8:16–17). Obviously, there were many organizational needs throughout the churches Paul planted. The fact that Titus was so enthusiastic about taking responsibility for this particular ministry project is indicative of his passion for charitable giving to meet the needs of God's people.

Another indicator that Titus was motivated by the gift of giving is the impact his passion had on others. Once Titus initiated the giving campaign in Corinth, the church responded with an "eager willingness" to participate (2 Cor. 8:11; 9:2), becoming not only the first church to actually give, but also the first to "have the desire to do so" (8:10). Don't miss the fact that, as enthusiastic as this church was to give generously while Titus was with them, their passion seems to have quickly faded once he left. Most of chapter 8 is given to challenging the Corinthians to complete the work they started and honor the pledges they had made. Just as the presence of Titus, motivated by his gift of giving, spurred the church on to loving generosity, so his subsequent absence resulted in a stalled campaign. That is the impact and response we might expect from someone with this motivational gift.

A final, brief passage that hints at Titus' gift of giving occurs at the conclusion of Paul's letter to him:

> Do everything you can to help Zenas the lawyer and Apollos on their way and see that they have everything they need. Our people must learn to devote themselves to doing whatever is good, in order that they may provide for daily necessities and not live unproductive lives. (Titus 3:13–14)

Although this passage is less conclusive than those noted above, it points to another example of Paul encouraging Titus to lead Christians in the practice of generosity. Titus had been left by Paul at Crete to help organize the newly planted churches, appointing elders in each town (Titus 1:5), teaching sound doctrine (2:1) and instructing fellow believers in how to live as followers of Christ (3:1–11). In concluding this brief letter Paul notes that Zenas and Apollos will be passing through on their way to furthering the work of the church. Titus is reminded both to make sure they have adequate provisions for their journey (3:13) and to encourage the church in providing for the "daily necessities" of those who are devoted to vocational ministry (3:14).

In reading through Paul's letter to Titus, I was stuck by the extremely detailed instruction given with regard to Titus' other responsibilities—appointing/training elders (most of chapter 1), teaching sound doctrine (all of chapter 2) and instructing the saints (most of chapter 3). When instructing Titus in the matter of giving and encouraging personal generosity in others, however, two simple verses sufficed. Clearly, this was not an area that Paul was concerned about Titus being adequately prepared. Why not? It is because Titus had successfully demonstrated his passion for giving, along with his desire and ability to motivate others in this vital area, during their work together in the church at Corinth.

Many a modern church and ministry has found it necessary to undertake a major giving campaign. New churches need to be built; the poor need food, clothing and medical care; the Bible needs to be translated into every language; the Gospel is to be preached and disciples made throughout the world. Such campaigns generally involve the appointment of someone to take the lead, both to oversee sound instruction in biblical stewardship principles and to encourage the grace of generous giving among God's people. Matthew and Titus stand as models for this important work: Matthew for his consistent instruction in the area of stewardship as taught by Jesus Himself, and Titus for his desire to roll up his sleeves and take the lead in motivating the saints to give freely and cheerfully to this important work.

The "Dark Side" of the Gift of Giving

It doesn't take too much imagination to guess the characteristics of the giving gift operating in the flesh. Folks with the motivational gift of giving are generous by nature; giving away large portions of their income is as natural as eating or breathing. Since they find it so easy to respond when funds are being raised for ministry, they can quickly start to feel pretty good about themselves when they give first or most, or when they are recognized publicly for their generosity.

The carnal giver might be tempted by the campaign that promises a personalized plaque on the wall, the recognition plate on the pew or their name memorialized on the new hospital wing. Whereas the giver walking in the Spirit will choose anonymity; the giver walking in the flesh is high-risk to seek attention and accolades. They might publicly attempt to deflect some of the attention, but inwardly they'll find satisfaction in it.

Another temptation faced by the carnal giver is the tendency toward a critical spirit. This can occur when fundraising targets are not being met for a particular ministry project; the person with the motivational gift of giving can become very condemning of other church members or ministry partners for not pulling their own weight. Worse, this gift in the flesh can find itself criticizing the financial decisions made by others.

If the giver has chosen to always drive a used car, for example, he will become privately indignant when someone he perceives is giving less purchases a new car. If a person or couple is struggling financially, the giver may quickly judge them for their lack of generosity and faithful handling of God's money. The generous giver must take care not to see herself as the standard for Christian giving and begin to judge others accordingly.

A third characteristic of the flesh perverting the motivational gift of giving is an ungrateful heart. As mentioned earlier, since givers love to give, they will frequently control or minimize their personal lifestyle in order to be able to give more. When walking in the flesh they can develop an ungodly disdain for God's material blessings. A needed move to a larger home in order to accommodate a growing family might be refused in the name of good stewardship. Family vacations might be avoided, seen as unnecessary and detrimental to the cause of giving more money to God's work. At its extreme, this gift operating in the flesh will begin to measure people's spiritual maturity by their abandonment of material possessions and the simplicity of their lifestyle. This trap will completely rob the giver of joy, either as she exercises the gift of giving and/or of the enjoyment of the many blessings our loving Father provides for His people.

SUMMARIZING THE GIFT OF GIVING

What an incredible blessing to God's people is the motivational gift of giving when operating in the Spirit! Christian missionaries are preaching and living the Gospel throughout the world, largely funded by the abundant financial support of those with this gift. Churches, homeless shelters and addiction recovery centers; justice ministries, rehabilitated housing and food pantries; Bible translations and teaching materials; seminaries and leadership training facilities—so much of the investment needed to advance the cause of Christ around the world—are largely being funded by those saints whom God has divinely enabled to give generously.

The person gifted in this way will give graciously and cheerfully, and often encourages the grace of liberal giving among those around them. They are frequently excellent stewards of God's resources and will often make do with less in order to give more. They feel most alive, and sense God's pleasure, when using the resources He's entrusted to them to fund an important ministry cause in Jesus' name.

Those with the motivational gift of giving find that trusting in God's provision for all their needs is second nature. They are never concerned about giving too much away; they know the ultimate Giver and trust in His glorious promise of provision: "I have never seen the righteous forsaken or their children begging bread" (Psalm 37:25). The giver is often blessed with an ability to generate excess and/or additional sources of income in order to give more generously to God's work around the world.

Does your heart beat more intensely when there is a call to raise funds for an important ministry work? Do you find your greatest joy in being able to meet the financial needs of God's people? Is your idea of the ultimate shopping spree the giving of a large year-end financial gift and getting to decide which worthy ministries to divide it among? Do you eagerly anticipate writing charitable checks, and feel most fulfilled after having done so? If you've answered some of these questions in the affirmative, it may well be that God has blessed you with the motivational gift of giving.

CHAPTER FOURTEEN

The Motivational Gift of Leadership

"If it is leadership, let him govern diligently."

ROMANS 12:8

The motivational gift of leadership is a wonderful thing to behold in the body of Christ. In fact, very little effective ministry will be accomplished in the local church if those with this gift are not encouraged to lead. Elder and deacon boards, ministries and committees, various projects and church functions, all run much more smoothly when facilitated by someone with the gift of leadership. The Greek word translated "lead" (nasb) or "leadership" (niv) in Romans 12:8 is prohistemi, a word that conveys the picture of someone standing out front (i.e., leading) or presiding over others (i.e., ruling, governing).

> DEFINITION: The motivational gift of leadership is God's enablement to lead, manage or govern His people, often involving casting vision, motivating and directing people to work in unity to accomplish a God-given purpose.

The gift of leadership might well be the most misunderstood of the seven motivational gifts. This is true because we tend to mistake some unrelated factors for the gift of leadership. For example, in the church people have a tendency to confuse vocation with spiritual gifting. When someone joins the church and his employment responsibilities include managing others or business ownership, he will frequently be guided toward a position of leadership in the church when he expresses the desire to serve. It will be assumed that, since he is successful in a leadership role at work, he must be gifted by God to serve as a leader in the local church.

In reality, vocational experience has no bearing on the motivational gift God has imparted to a believer. And this tendency often results in leader burnout as one with no internal motivation or gift to lead quickly becomes frustrated and drained in his ministry service.

Another unrelated factor often mistaken for the leadership gift—as is true with the prophetic gift—is one's personality. Someone with a strong personality and people skills, or someone who insists on being in control, will frequently be elevated to a position of leadership in the church regardless of his or her actual gifting. The modern-day church is frequently plagued by a lack of motivated volunteers, so those who indicate a desire to be in charge of a ministry are frequently (and enthusiastically) granted their wish, often with disastrous results. Many a ministry has folded, often leaving in its wake a line of damaged saints, because church members with no leadership ability have proactively moved into key positions in the church.

It is an immense blessing, however, when those God has gifted to lead are identified, trained and encouraged in the exercise of their motivational gift.

CHARACTERISTICS

One of the key characteristics of the person with the motivational gift of leadership is the ability to motivate others in their ministry service. It has been said that those with the leadership gift tend to bring out the best in others. They help to elevate the ministry performance of those around them by trusting their team members enough to delegate important tasks and responsibilities. They often expect a lot from others, but their confidence in others is what causes team members to excel, to rally to the cause and go above and beyond the call of duty. Whereas ministry leaders lacking this gift will often have to "motivate" others by complaining, cajoling or making team members feel guilty, folks serving in ministry tend to serve joyfully and enthusiastically when following a gifted leader.

Another important characteristic of the leadership gift is the ability to provide a sound plan and direction for ministry. The leader may or may not be the primary visionary, but once he understands what the ultimate objective is for a ministry initiative he can quickly envision the means of accomplishing the goal, including the various support positions that will need to be filled. Leaders have an uncanny ability to see the big picture and break even the biggest of projects down to its component parts. The leader will then effectively recruit church members into support positions and provide the oversight and direction needed for the successful accomplishment of the task at hand.

For those of us who do not have this gift, some of our most blessed ministry experiences have involved serving under someone with the gift of leadership. In fact, even in cases where the ministry itself wasn't something we were particularly passionate about, the service was enjoyable and fruitful because of our experience with the leader. The gifted leader instills confidence in her followers, and makes the work of ministry enjoyable even when the going gets tough. They also help others to see—even to feel—the vital importance of their effort. They are able to help people focus on the results and impact of their ministry service.

The person with the motivational gift of leadership will also personally model the values of the ministry. They lead by example, which is why people are quick to follow. Gifted leaders are both confident and humble, their confidence being in God's ability to accomplish His work and their humility emanating from an intimate relationship with Christ. The leader does not seek attention or praise; he is driven instead by a desire for kingdom advancement and to see lives impacted for Christ as a result of his service.

The leader establishes goals for the ministry or project and takes personal responsibility for their accomplishment. Should the project fall behind schedule or important deadlines be missed, the leader will take full responsibility and consider it her personal failing. This rarely occurs, however, because their commitment to action, and to leading by example, inspires their team members to a high level of achievement. On the other hand, when all goes according to plan and the mission has been accomplished, the leader is quick to first give glory to God and then to acknowledge the committed and valuable work of the team.

The gifted leader has no need of personal accolades or attention, and rarely dwells for long on any ministry success. There is always a new work to be done, a new ministry initiative to be implemented, and the leader thrives on moving on to the next ministry challenge.

The gifted leader will often become more influential than he desires, not because he pursues positions of influence but because people become accustomed to following his lead. They are diligent, determined and passionate about their work for the Lord. They are decisive, never shying away from making difficult decisions and always willing to deal with the consequences. The leader is often a self-starter with regard to ministry assignments and has an orientation toward goal-setting. The leader is persuasive but not manipulative, driven but not without compassion.

Like Jesus, the most effective outworking of this motivational gift is the humble, servant leader. The gifted leader never takes for granted those he is responsible to lead. He understands his role as mentor, shepherd and friend. The leader will not consider a ministry task to have been successfully accomplished unless the team has grown and matured through the process. It is never just about achieving the stated results; the leader is motivated to guide her team members into a more intimate relationship with Jesus through the process. Helping people mature in their faith is just as important to the leader as completing the work assigned.

THE GIFT OF LEADERSHIP IN JESUS

Human history has never known a more perfect, gifted and effective leader than Jesus of Nazareth. The strength of His character and convictions led Him to give "Himself [His life] as a ransom for all men" (1 Tim. 2:6); His humility and servant's heart continue to motivate loving, sacrificial service throughout the world in His name. What was the attitude of this great leader of men, and what should be our attitude in response?

> Your attitude should be the same as that of Christ Jesus: Who, being in very nature God, did not consider equality with God something to be grasped, but made himself nothing, taking the very nature of a servant, being made in human likeness. And being found in appearance as a man, he humbled himself and became obedient to death—even death on a cross! (Phil. 2:5–8)

As noted above, an important outworking of the leadership gift is humility. Following the lead of his Lord and Savior, the person with the motivational gift of leadership is first of all a humble servant. He expects others to follow him only as he follows Christ. Though his ministry service usually bears fruit—abundant fruit—he considers himself to be nothing more than a grateful servant of his King.

Another characteristic of this gift modeled by Jesus is leading by example. Note the progression of events recorded at the beginning of chapters 8, 9 and 10 of Luke's gospel:

> After this, Jesus traveled about from one town and village to another, proclaiming the good news of the kingdom of God. The Twelve were with him, and also some women who had been cured of evil spirits and diseases. (Luke 8:1–2)

> When Jesus had called the Twelve together, he gave them power and authority to drive out all demons and to cure diseases, and he sent them out to preach the kingdom of God and to heal the sick. So they set out and went from village to village, preaching the gospel and healing people everywhere. (Luke 9:1–2, 6)

> After this the Lord appointed seventy-two others and sent them two by two ahead of him to every town and place where he was

> about to go. "Heal the sick who are there and tell them, 'The kingdom of God is near you.'" (Luke 10:1, 9)

Jesus spent the early years of His ministry healing the sick, casting out demons and preaching the Gospel. Then, when He deemed the time to be right, Jesus sent out His closest twelve to do likewise. Finally, once His inner circle had carried out the work He had modeled and for which He had prepared them, Jesus sent out the larger group of His followers to do the same. Is this not the precise method Jesus used to establish and expand the New Testament church through the ministry of Paul, Peter and others?

Gifted leaders lead by example. They don't expect anyone to do work they are not willing to do themselves. Though a delegator by nature and necessity, the leader never hesitates to roll up her sleeves and work alongside her team members. Like Jesus, she models the values of the ministry and then invites team members to do likewise.

I mentioned earlier in this chapter that the leader stays focused on the big picture and helps others do the same. A corresponding example of Jesus' gift of leadership occurs in the fourth chapter of Luke's gospel, a time when the apostles thought Jesus should stay in town and enjoy His popularity and the attention He was getting:

> When the sun was setting, the people brought to Jesus all who had various kinds of sickness, and laying his hands on each one, he healed them. Moreover, demons came out of many people, shouting, "You are the Son of God!" But he rebuked them and would not allow them to speak, because they knew he was the Christ. At daybreak Jesus went out to a solitary place. The people were looking for him and when they came to where he was, they tried to keep him from leaving them. But he said, "I must preach the good news of the kingdom of God to the other towns also, because that is why I was sent." (Luke 4:40–43)

Luke tells us that when Jesus' followers found Him the next morning, they "tried to keep Him from leaving." Would we not have done the same? Jesus had already been rejected at Nazareth, the crowd in the synagogue having tried to kill Him after He publicly announced that He was the long-awaited Messiah (Luke 4:28–29). Then His followers encountered a decidedly more positive ministry experience: People were streaming to Jesus as He graciously healed their sick and cast out demons. Acceptance at last! Who wouldn't want to hang around and soak in the moment?

So appreciative and impressed were those who witnessed Jesus' ministry the prior evening that, the next morning, the crowd's primary objective was to find Jesus and keep Him from leaving. Though His apostles appear to have been in agreement with this plan, Jesus refused to allow the adoring crowds to distract Him from the larger goal: to preach the Good News to neighboring towns. Jesus didn't come to enjoy personal popularity and attention; He came to save His people from their sins (Matt. 1:21). What an important lesson for Peter and the other disciples—the future leaders of Christ's church—to learn very early in their walk with Jesus! We are not here for our own glory. We're here to preach the Gospel and advance the cause of Christ in the world.

Jesus taught His followers to stay focused on the bigger picture: the redemption of those who are lost and without hope. He embodied strength and humility, and He led by example. Those endowed with the motivational gift of leadership are similarly focused, and they encourage those they lead to do the same.

The Gift of Leadership in Others

An excellent example of the motivational gift of leadership in the New Testament is the apostle Peter. Although Peter was part of Jesus' inner circle, after Jesus' crucifixion he was among those least likely to ever rise to a position of leadership in Christ's church. Peter had a tendency to be impulsive and abrasive, often making inappropriate comments at important times (Luke 9:33; Matt. 16:22–23; John 13:8; Matt. 26:33, 35) that required Jesus' rebuke. On the night that Jesus was arrested, outspoken

Peter, having earlier the same evening promised allegiance unto death, publicly denied ever knowing Jesus.

Peter denied Jesus with his words, then "with an oath," and finally with "curses" (Matt. 26:69–74). Appropriately, after remembering that Jesus had predicted these very actions, Peter "went outside and wept bitterly" (Matt. 26:75). It is doubtful whether Jesus' disciples would have been anxious to follow Peter at that point in his life, and perhaps even more doubtful that he felt qualified to lead. Thankfully, the risen Christ refused to leave Peter to wallow in self-pity or to allow his ministry potential to be nullified by his public failure.

After the Holy Spirit came at Pentecost, Peter's leadership in the early church became well-established. Jesus had implied on several occasions that He intended for Peter to have an important leadership role in His church (Mark 1:17; Matt. 16:16–19; John 21:15–17). The outpouring of the Holy Spirit at Pentecost provided the necessary gifting for this work. Peter's sermon at Pentecost was a defining moment in his life, establishing him as a key leader and spokesman for Jesus and demonstrating a gifted leader's ability to motivate people to action:

> Peter replied, "Repent and be baptized, every one of you, in the name of Jesus Christ for the forgiveness of your sins. And you will receive the gift of the Holy Spirit. The promise is for you and your children and for all who are far off—for all whom the Lord our God will call." With many other words he warned them; and he pleaded with them, "Save yourselves from this corrupt generation." Those who accepted his message were baptized, **and about three thousand were added to their number that day**. (Acts 2:38–41 emphasis mine)

> The priests and the captain of the temple guard and the Sadducees came up to Peter and John while they were speaking to the people. They were greatly disturbed because the apostles were teaching the people and proclaiming in Jesus the resurrec-

> tion of the dead. They seized Peter and John, and because it was evening, they put them in jail until the next day. But many who heard the message believed, **and the number of men grew to about five thousand.** (Acts 4:1–4 emphasis mine)

It is interesting to me that Peter's preaching frequently resulted in mass conversions to Christ. When he took the Gospel for the first time to the Gentiles (at Cornelius' house in Acts 10), every person present who heard his message came to faith in Christ and received the Holy Spirit. It would be fair to say that, prior to this time, Peter was not someone people were likely to follow, or someone with an ability to inspire large groups of people to action. However, guided by the gifting of the indwelling Holy Spirit, he preached the Gospel and people quickly responded to his leading.

As Peter led the apostles and the apostles led the people, we see a clear ministry direction in the church from its infancy. Under Peter's leadership the newly converted followers of Christ begin to meet regularly for worship, teaching, prayer and fellowship (Acts 2). Peter sets the example for the other leaders with the first recorded healing in the new church (Acts 3), modeling how to deflect attention from self and focus it rightly on Jesus. He picks up where Jesus left off in condemning the religious elite for their rejection of the Messiah and leading the people astray (Acts 4). He institutes the first example of church discipline with Ananias and Sapphira (Acts 5). He oversees, along with the other apostles, the appointing of the first deacons, an action taken to allow the leaders to remain focused on their primary mission (Acts 6). As noted above, Peter was used by God to open the door of the Gospel both to the Jews and to the Gentiles.

When Saul of Tarsus was converted to Christ and commissioned to preach the Gospel to the Gentiles, it is Peter that he first sought to become acquainted with (Gal. 1:18). When there was a dispute at Antioch between Jewish and Gentile converts, Peter led the council at Jerusalem that was convened to resolve the disagreement.

One of the easiest ways to identify someone with the gift of leadership is that people follow them. The gift of leadership is different from positional authority. Many people are put it positions of authority, and subordinates will often be obedient to their direction because it is their responsibility to do so—whether or not they like, trust or respect the leader. Folks with the motivational gift of leadership, however, don't have to seek followers; followers find them. Note that Jesus didn't have to try hard to draw a crowd. When calling the disciples, His recruiting method consisted of a simple request: Follow me. Peter, Andrew, Matthew, et al, dropped everything and followed Jesus. Leaders attract devoted followers.

Gifted leaders find themselves continually being placed in positions of leadership, even when they aren't seeking such positions. This is how it was with Peter post-Pentecost. He became influential, persuasive, decisive and determined. He was passionate for the mission, and he directed those he was leading to their respective roles in furthering the cause. Despite the various skirmishes that arose during his ministry—dissension from Jewish leaders, imprisonment and disagreement within the local church—Peter was able to stay firmly focused on the bigger picture of spreading the Gospel.

Another New Testament example of the gift of leadership is James, the half-brother of Jesus. Prior to coming to faith in Christ, the only account we have of James is not a very flattering one. Mary's other sons included James, Joseph, Simon and Judas (Matt. 13:55). Mark's gospel describes a time when Jesus' family members "went to take charge of him, for they said, 'He is out of his mind.'" (Mark 3:21). John's gospel notes that Jesus' "brothers did not believe in him" (John 7:5). Transformation occurred, however, after the risen Christ appeared to His brother, James (noted in 1 Cor. 15:7).

The converted James became a prominent leader in the early church. It is evident that James was already in leadership at the church in Jerusalem by the time Saul of Tarsus came to faith (Gal. 1:19). He remained in this position through Paul's last trip through Jerusalem (Acts 21:18). When Peter was miraculously freed from prison by an angel and went to the home of John Mark where some of the faithful had gathered to pray, he specifically instructed those present to "tell James and the brothers about this" (Acts 12:17). Along with Peter, James was also among those who presided over the council at Jerusalem (Acts 15). It was James, in fact, who proposed the resolution that was ultimately adopted by the other leaders. Clearly, James was a highly respected leader in the early church; Paul referred to him as a "pillar" of the church in Galatians 2:9.

A gifted leader has an ability to always keep the bigger picture in focus. Consider James' influence during the proceedings of the council at Jerusalem. After the issues in dispute had been laid out and "the apostles and elders met to consider this question" (Acts 15:6), Peter, presumably representing the apostles, spoke first, and James, most likely representing the elders, spoke last. When an important decision needed to be made at this critical point in the church's history, James is the one the other leaders looked to. The biblical account records James speaking only once, at the very end of the discussion. That the other leaders immediately agreed with his summary and recommendation indicates that James was a man of profound influence. The wisdom he shared in proposing a resolution demonstrates his focus on the big picture of continuing to advance the Gospel.

We identified humility in service as one of the characteristics of the motivational gift of leadership. One might expect James to have made a point of highlighting his formal relation to Jesus—they were brothers, both sons of Mary—either to exert some authority or to increase his personal influence. It is interesting that in the epistle bearing his name and authorship, James introduces himself only as "James, a servant of God and of the Lord Jesus Christ" (James 1:1). The only church leader who was directly related to Jesus was James; yet in his humility he sees himself only as a grateful servant of his Lord.

Eusebius (c. AD 260–339), bishop of Caesarea and the first Christian historian, notes a prior writer's contention that James was known as "the Just" due to his personal piety and holiness. If true, that would align with Paul's view of James as a "pillar" in the church, and it would speak to the issue of James' leadership by example. His epistle encourages Christians in a wide array of godly behavior; it is appropriate that James sought first to live out these views before men, and then to exhort other to do the same.

THE "DARK SIDE" OF THE GIFT OF LEADERSHIP

As valuable and important as is the leadership gift to the body of Christ, there are several areas of caution that warrant discussion. A leader operating in the flesh, if not careful, can be reduced to a heartless dictator, ordering team members around with no thought to their feelings or growth. The flesh craves power, and the leader is usually in the unique position of exercising great authority in the church. Those with the motivational gift of leadership must always guard against the temptation to use their position to lord it over their team members.

Another challenge faced by the gifted leader walking in the flesh is politicking. Church leadership teams are generally made up of folks with different personalities and spiritual gifts. Since the gift of leadership is only present in a minority of folks in church leadership, those so gifted can become easily frustrated by the performance of those around them. Basic leadership skills—planning, goal-setting, decisiveness, determination—come naturally to gifted leaders, so they often find it hard to understand why everyone else isn't wired the same way. This can lead to the leader trying to build a following of folks who are sympathetic with his views in an attempt to circumvent the leadership structure in the church. Because the leader is highly respected, this practice will usually succeed, much to the detriment of the church and its other leaders. Factions will quickly arise, creating an environment of suspicion and distrust. Whereas the leader walking in the Spirit is humble, patient, and a team-builder, the leader walking in the flesh can become a destructive force on a leadership team.

Perhaps the greatest challenge faced by the fleshly leader, however, is overcommitment. Most gifted leaders have an unusually high capacity for work. They are often able to manage multiple ministry tasks at the same time. Since they become highly visible in the local church because they are frequently spearheading important projects, they are the ones most likely to be invited to help on other projects and committees. In fact, as they become known, these leaders are also pursued for positions in parachurch organizations and local nonprofits. The fleshly leader believes he can fix any problem and improve any ministry. This mindset, combined with the excitement they feel when attacking a new ministry problem, often leads to their agreeing to serve in an unmanageable number of ministries.

When a leader has overcommitted, unpleasant things happen. Those commitments for which they have no passion will start to drain their emotional energy. Serving will become a "have to." They'll find it difficult to focus on the work because of their lack of interest and feeling of resentment. Rather than simply acknowledging their overcommitment and making the decision to resign from some of the ministries, they'll insist on pressing on; leaders don't like to back out of commitments, no matter how distasteful they've become. Serving in too many ministries will eventually rob the leader of their joy in serving in any of the ministries, even those for which there is a strong passion.

Overcommitted leaders are at high risk for leadership burnout. All who have the motivational gift of leadership would be well-advised to have several accountability partners, close friends who love them enough to be painfully honest. This practice will help the leader to consistently walk in the Spirit and to avoid becoming overcommitted.

A final word of caution to those with the motivational gift of leadership: Choose wisely those ministries or projects to which you commit yourself. Gifted leaders love new projects. They are energized both by creative ministry ideas and committees in need of revival. The leader is good at both, and so tends to say yes to such opportunities without much thought, counsel or prayer. When a ministry is struggling or "broken," the leadership gift can immediately identify several ways to fix the problems. When a new vision is cast, the leader can readily identify the steps that need to be taken in order to bring the ministry to life. As a result, the leader operating in the flesh will frequently bounce from ministry to ministry, never staying in one endeavor long enough to see it through to completion.

This habit is different from overcommitment in that the leader may well only be involved in one ministry at a time. The problem is the tendency to say yes to things for which they have no passion, or for ministries that really need to be terminated for lack of interest.

Churches are notorious for keeping unnecessary and unproductive ministries on life-support. Gifted leaders operating in the flesh will frequently agree to take over such ministries, expecting to breathe new life into them. In the absence of any passion for the ministry, or a sense of purpose (the leader will quickly recognize when a ministry project is serving no purpose), the leader will phase out of the work, taking with him great feelings of guilt. This cycle can repeat itself over and over, with a qualified and gifted leader allowing his or her flesh to render the gift useless. If you have the motivational gift of leadership and have found yourself bouncing aimlessly from one ministry to another, my encouragement is to choose wisely which opportunities you agree to take on. This is another area in which the counsel of accountability partners is invaluable.

Summarizing the Gift of Leadership

Remember that the biblical word "leadership," as it appears in the original language, connotes both a leading and ruling function. Those with the motivational gift of leadership are most easily identified by the tendency of others to follow them. Leaders are able to pull a team together and encourage each member to excellence in service. The leader is humble, influential, confident, decisive and persuasive, a motivator of those with whom he is serving. He brings out the best in fellow team members, who feel more like they're working "with" him rather than "for" him.

The leader is a natural delegator but always leads first by example. She is trustworthy, determined and passionate for the mission. She is a self-starter and goal-setter, diligent in her work and focused on developing her team members. The gifted leader is adept at breaking a large ministry objective down into its component parts and recruiting the people needed for each part. Under a gifted leader's steady hand, team members grow and mature through the ministry process, and ministry goals and objectives are consistently achieved.

A leader will model the values of the ministry. His teams are enthusiastic about their work, unified in their approach, joyful in their service.

Do you find yourself frequently being placed in positions of leadership even when you aren't actively seeking them? Do ministry team members often look to you when important or difficult decisions need to be made? Do people tend to follow you without any prompting, and to become highly motivated for ministry service when in your presence?

When you hear of a new ministry objective, does your mind begin to race and your heart rate increase as you immediately begin to formulate a plan for implementation? When you see an important ministry project languishing, are you able to quickly identify the several steps needed to breathe life back into it? Are you persuasive without being manipulative, influential without seeking power? If you can answer in the affirmative for some or most of these questions, it is probable that God has blessed you with the motivational gift of leadership.

Chapter Fifteen

The Motivational Gift of Mercy

"If it is showing mercy, let him do it cheerfully."

Romans 12:8

Throughout the history of the church, countless lives have been touched by the loving exercise of the motivational gift of mercy. Wherever there is pain, poverty and disease, there you'll find those with the mercy gift offering food, clothing, shelter and medical care, all in the name of their merciful King. Where there is human suffering of any kind the mercy gift is visibly active, bringing comfort and healing in Jesus' name.

Followers of Jesus are commanded not only to preach the Gospel, but also to live it out. Few do so with greater love and compassion than those He has endowed with the motivational gift of mercy.

> Definition: The motivational gift of mercy is God's enablement to joyfully meet the needs of those who are suffering physically, mentally or emotionally, by demonstrating Christ's love in visible and practical ways.

It is important to note that the Greek word for mercy in Romans 12:8 connotes more than simply *feeling* mercy or compassion toward those in need; there is also the sense of *acting* on those feelings. Definitions include: to have mercy on, to help one afflicted, and to bring help.

I point this out because it is not at all unusual for a follower of Christ to feel great compassion for those who are suffering and in need. However, most of us are rarely moved by those feelings to take action to eliminate the suffering. We applaud the Mother Theresas of the world and admire those ministering to the homeless in our cities, but we aren't quick to personally participate in such ministries of mercy.

Not so with folks who possess this motivational gift. Those with the gift of mercy are compelled to act, doing whatever they can to bring relief to human pain and suffering.

Characteristics

Those with the motivational gift of mercy feel exceptional compassion and empathy toward those who are suffering. They weep with those who weep and mourn with those who mourn (Rom. 12:15), feeling their anguish at a deep personal level. They truly reflect the heart of Jesus when encountering someone in need.

People with the mercy gift are not only intent on alleviating the pain and discomfort in suffering people; they are also moved to find ways to eliminate the sources of such pain. Folks with the gift of mercy are more apt to open a soup kitchen than provide a one-time meal. After all, they reason, those who are hungry today will likely be the same tomorrow. People with the mercy gift cannot tolerate such ongoing suffering, and they are compelled to provide longer-term solutions to these problems. They will often take part in spearheading major changes in social policy or the establishment of new social initiatives in local government in order to eliminate the debilitating social ills in their communities.

It is not only physical needs that move a person with the mercy gift. Emotional pain in others, such as loneliness, grieving or sadness, will also attract the loving care of one with the gift of mercy. They will provide friendship, a sympathetic ear or gentle encouragement, doing anything they can to relieve the pain.

Those with the mercy gift are great listeners because they are truly interested in connecting at a heart level with those they serve. Perhaps more than any other motivational gift, the mercy gift is selfless in its application, sincerely living out Paul's instruction in Philippians 2:3: "Do nothing out of selfish ambition or vain conceit, but in humility consider others better than yourselves."

Regardless of the particular plight of those who are suffering—or the reason for their condition—the person with the mercy gift expresses love, grace and dignity to those in need. The gift of mercy does not judge (see Matt. 7:1–2) those who are in need, nor does it look condescendingly on those whose behavior or decisions have caused their plight. Those with the mercy gift are keenly aware that everyone is equal in that all are created in the image of God (Gen. 1:27). They treat the suffering with utmost dignity because they sincerely value every human being.

Folks with the motivational gift of mercy are often willing to serve in unsightly locations and the most difficult of circumstances. What's more, they will do so cheerfully, grateful for the opportunity to be used by God to bring the love of Christ into a place where few Christians are likely to go. Those with the mercy gift are empathetic, caring, compassionate and kind. They are responsive, sensitive and gentle, quick to bear the burdens of others.

The practical love and compassion of Jesus are rarely displayed more clearly, or more compellingly, than when the mercy gift is being manifested in His name.

The Gift of Mercy in Jesus

Jesus Christ so readily demonstrated the gift of mercy that it is difficult to choose just a few examples. In so many instances, Jesus did something because He was motivated by compassion (Matt. 9:36; 14:14; 15:32; 20:34; Mark 1:41; 6:34; 8:2; Luke 7:13). It is interesting that, in all of these cases, Jesus' feelings of compassion led to action: preaching the Gospel, healing their diseases, feeding the hungry, teaching His Word, casting out demons, even raising a widow's son from the dead. Jesus was the very embodiment of mercy; His heartfelt compassion toward those in need always moved Him to loving action.

One particular passage that depicts Jesus' gift of mercy is Matthew 14:13–21:

> When Jesus heard what had happened, he withdrew by boat privately to a solitary place. Hearing of this, the crowds followed him on foot from the towns. When Jesus landed and saw a large crowd, he had compassion on them and healed their sick. As evening approached, the disciples came to him and said, "This is a remote place, and it's already getting late. Send the crowds away, so they can go to the villages and buy themselves some food."
>
> Jesus replied, "They do not need to go away. You give them something to eat."
>
> "We have here only five loaves of bread and two fish," they answered. "Bring them here to me," he said. And he directed the people to sit down on the grass. Taking the five loaves and the two fish and looking up to heaven, he gave thanks and broke the loaves. Then he gave them to the disciples, and the disciples gave them to the people. They all ate and were satisfied, and the disciples picked up twelve basketfuls of broken pieces that were left over. The number of those who ate was about five thousand men, besides women and children.

A very important aspect of Jesus' compassion is often overlooked in this passage because of its focus on the miraculous feeding of the crowd. Considering the broader context, however, reveals the depth of Jesus' care for those in need. Note verse 13: "When Jesus heard what had happened." What is it that had happened? It was the violent murder of John the Baptist, Jesus' cousin and friend, the one whom the Scriptures foretold would go before Messiah to prepare the way. Let us remember that Jesus was both fully God and fully man. In his humanity, He was subject to the same emotions that we are.

We know that Jesus felt sadness; He wept at Lazarus' tomb and over Jerusalem as He entered the city. We can reasonably surmise that He was distraught at the news that John had been murdered, beheaded at the hands of Herod. Jesus responded to this horrible news in much the same way we all deal with tragedy: He withdrew privately to a solitary place. Jesus was grieving and He wanted to be alone.

Safe to say the crowd did not respond to Jesus' grief with the same compassion He would soon demonstrate toward them. When the crowd heard of this, rather than allow Jesus a rare time of privacy, they followed along on foot to where His boat was headed. When His boat landed and He saw the large crowd awaiting His arrival, what was His response? Anger, frustration or contempt? No. Did He chastise the crowd for infringing on His privacy, or send them away so He could be left alone to grieve? Not Jesus. "He had compassion on them and healed their sick" (v. 14).

Jesus' actions in this passage give us great insight into the gift of mercy. Even in the midst of personal pain and suffering, the person with the mercy gift will quickly forget about self when faced with someone else's suffering. Despite the pain in His own heart at the loss of John, Jesus spent that afternoon healing the sick and the evening providing food, making sure that no one left without having their needs met.

Another clear example of Jesus exercising the gift of mercy occurs in Luke 7:11–15:

> Soon afterward, Jesus went to a town called Nain, and his disciples and a large crowd went along with him. As he approached the town gate, a dead person was being carried out—the only son of his mother, and she was a widow. And a large crowd from the town was with her. When the Lord saw her, his heart went out to her and he said, "Don't cry." Then he went up and touched the coffin, and those carrying it stood still. He said, "Young man, I say to you, get up!" The dead man sat up and began to talk, and Jesus gave him back to his mother.

One of the most striking things about Jesus' mercy and compassion is that He felt the pain of others at the deepest personal level, even when He knew He was going to eliminate their suffering. As noted above, Jesus wept at the tomb of His dear friend, Lazarus (John 11:35), even though He was about to bring him back to life. In the account of the widow's son, as Jesus observed the grief and mourning of a widow who had lost her only son, Jesus shared in her grief even though He was about to miraculously end her suffering. Those possessing the motivational gift of mercy understand these feelings of Jesus all too well.

You may remember the Old Testament law's prohibition against a Jew coming into contact with a dead body (Num. 19:11). The risk of becoming ceremonially unclean did not hinder Jesus from touching the coffin. This example might be similar to a Christian being willing to serve in unsanitary, unsightly conditions in order to physically minister to the poverty-stricken and diseased.

Note also Jesus' act of giving the son back to his mother. His merciful deed did not end with Jesus raising the dead man to life. This encounter was about the grieving mother. It was she to whom "his heart went out" (Luke 7:13), she that was experiencing deep grief and loss. Indeed, Jesus' demonstration of mercy toward this widow could only be completed by His personally giving the resurrected son back to his mother.

Think of all the attention that must have been focused on Jesus at that moment. He walked toward Nain's city gate leading a very large crowd of followers; He stopped the funeral procession by walking up and touching the coffin, an act unthinkable for a Jew; He raised a dead man before their eyes. The crowds must have been awestruck and filled with inexpressible joy. The attention of both crowds, those following Jesus and those in the funeral procession, would surely have been focused on Jesus. But where was Jesus' focus? From beginning to end of this encounter, Jesus' attention remained firmly on the one who was suffering. His heart went out to her, His mercy and compassion inevitably moving Him to action. Jesus relieved her pain in a way that only He could, and He lovingly restored her joy by giving her son back to her.

Perhaps the most notable example of Jesus' mercy and compassion, however, was His crucifixion. I refer not only to the obvious—Jesus sacrificial (and painful) death on our behalf in order that we might be reconciled to God—but His actions toward His persecutors: "Father, forgive them, for they do not know what they are doing." (Luke 23:34)

Think through all that He faced during the week leading up to the actual crucifixion: betrayed by one of His own; the crowd of once enthusiastic followers having mostly turned on Him; abandoned by His apostles; convicted on false charges; stripped, beaten, kicked, punched and spat upon; speared in the side while hanging on a cross between two convicted thieves; suffering the physical pain of the most brutal form of execution; and abandoned by His Father as His wrath was being poured out for our sins.

This Jesus, on the verge of breathing His last, calls upon His Father in heaven seeking mercy for those who are responsible for His own suffering. As great as Jesus' personal pain and torment was, He quickly forgot Himself in order to plead for His Father's mercy toward others.

The Gift of Mercy in Others

One example of a follower of Jesus in the New Testament that appears to have been blessed with the gift of mercy is Dorcas. Though she is mentioned in only one section of the Bible (Acts 9:36–42), Luke's description includes several characteristics of the mercy gift.

> In Joppa there was a disciple named Tabitha (which, when translated, is Dorcas), who was always doing good and helping the poor. About that time she became sick and died, and her body was washed and placed in an upstairs room. Lydda was near Joppa; so when the disciples heard that Peter was in Lydda, they sent two men to him and urged him, "Please come at once!" Peter went with them, and when he arrived he was taken upstairs to the room. All the widows stood around him, crying and showing him the robes and other clothing that Dorcas had made while she was still with them.
>
> Peter sent them all out of the room; then he got down on his

> knees and prayed. Turning toward the dead woman, he said, "Tabitha, get up." She opened her eyes, and seeing Peter she sat up. He took her by the hand and helped her to her feet. Then he called the believers and the widows and presented her to them alive. This became known all over Joppa, and many people believed in the Lord.

We know that Dorcas was a "disciple" of Christ and, therefore, indwelt by the Holy Spirit. Though little information is given in this brief account, Luke chose to highlight that she "was always doing good and helping the poor" (v. 36). If these are the traits by which Dorcas was best known in her hometown of Joppa, little wonder that her passing brought such sadness to those who knew her well.

Note the response of the widows present when Peter arrived. They gathered around Peter, "crying and showing him the robes and other clothing that Dorcas had made while she was still with them" (v. 39). I noted in an earlier chapter my contention that Luke, clearly possessing the motivational gift of teaching, chose his words very carefully when conveying his accounts of the life of Christ and the early church. Accuracy and detail were important to Luke (Luke 1:1–4). It would follow, then, that the merciful acts of Dorcas were well-known as being characteristic of her life in Christ.

According to the *New Bible Dictionary*, Second Edition, "Dorcas was renowned for charity at the church in Joppa" (page 289). The three specific actions attributed to Dorcas—doing good, helping the poor and caring for widows—all reflect the typical behavior of one with the motivational gift of mercy. I would also suggest that the sadness accompanying her death, especially the urgent action of her friends in finding Peter and bringing him to her home, presumably in hopes of a miracle, are reflective of the response we might expect when one so compassionate and merciful passes away.

Reflect on the death of Mother Theresa during our lifetime and how millions grieved throughout the world. Few in human history have impacted so many through their display of Christlike love in action, the essence of living out the Gospel of Jesus Christ. Albeit on a much smaller and more local scale, this is the response we see among those who knew and loved the disciple Dorcas.

Another excellent example of the motivational gift of mercy in action comes from a fictional character in the New Testament: the Good Samaritan. My preference in describing the seven motivational gifts has been to use real people, flesh and blood Christians living post-Pentecost (after the pouring out of the Holy Spirit to indwell believers in Acts 2:1–13). However, this instructive parable that Jesus told paints such a flawless picture of Christian mercy in action that I couldn't resist using it in this section.

> In reply Jesus said: "A man was going down from Jerusalem to Jericho, when he fell into the hands of robbers. They stripped him of his clothes, beat him and went away, leaving him half dead. A priest happened to be going down the same road, and when he saw the man, he passed by on the other side. So too, a Levite, when he came to the place and saw him, passed by on the other side. But a Samaritan, as he traveled, came where the man was; and when he saw him, he took pity on him. He went to him and bandaged his wounds, pouring on oil and wine. Then he put the man on his own donkey, took him to an inn and took care of him. The next day he took out two silver coins and gave them to the innkeeper. 'Look after him,' he said, 'and when I return, I will reimburse you for any extra expense you may have.'" (Luke 10:30–35)

Though this well-known parable is loaded with material on which to teach, I'll confine my thoughts to those characteristics that are consistent with the mercy gifting. The first thing we notice is that Jesus' choice in this story was to have a Samaritan showing mercy to Jew. The animosity between these two groups has been well-documented. Had this been a real incident, it is hard to imagine someone less likely to provide assistance to a Jew in distress than a Samaritan. And yet, to the Samaritan, there doesn't seem to be any racial distinction; he sees only someone who is hurt and in great need. His compassion moves him immediately to action.

Perhaps more than any of the other motivational gifts, the mercy gift is exercised just as freely outside the church as in the church. Folks with this gift are grieved by human suffering in any form, and will always do anything they can to relieve it. There is no prejudice in the mercy gifting—not racial, social, denominational, or otherwise. When they look upon someone in distress they see only a valuable and precious life, created in the image of God and worthy of honor and respect. Like the Samaritan in Jesus' story, the person with the gift of mercy will help anyone, anywhere, any time.

The second characteristic worth noting is that the Samaritan's feelings of compassion —"he took pity on him" (v. 33)—moved him immediately to action. This fact virtually defines the gift of mercy. Many of us who follow Christ could look upon such distress and suffering but not even consider taking action. Though we would surely be impacted by seeing someone stripped and beaten, lying in the street, many of us would sooner reach for our cell phone and dial 911 than pull our car off the road and physically help. Justifying our actions because of the appointment we'd have to miss, the blood we would surely get all over our new suit, or the obvious personal danger (could the perpetrators still be lurking nearby, waiting for another hapless victim?), we would most likely continue on our way, calling for help (maybe) but not stopping to offer it. The person with the mercy gift, on the other hand, never stops at simply having pity on someone; their pity always leads immediately to compassionate action.

A third characteristic that must not be overlooked is the direct, physical nature of the mercy gift's involvement with someone in need. The Samaritan "went to him and bandaged his wounds, pouring on oil and wine. Then he put the man on his own donkey, took him to an inn and took care of him" (v. 34).

Upon seeing someone in such distress, the person with the gift of mercy would not be content to just call for help and wait for an ambulance to arrive. She's willing to get the victim's blood on her hands, her clothes, and on the seat of her car, in order to transport the wounded to safety. Like the Samaritan, her personal schedule ceases to exist the moment she encounters someone in need. She'll stay as long as is needed to provide comfort and relief. Should further assistance be required, personally or financially, she is more than willing to return.

The Good Samaritan made everything he had available to the one who was suffering: his oil and wine, his donkey, his money and his time. This is the heart of the mercy gift.

The "Dark Side" of the Gift of Mercy

You might be wondering if there could possibly be a "dark side" to the mercy gift. How could a motivational gift that displays such love, mercy and compassion toward others, that knows no prejudice and sees the inherent dignity and worth in all people, possibly have any downside? We must remember, however, that we continue to struggle with our flesh, and any gift of God that becomes subject to our flesh can be distorted. In the case of the mercy gift, acting in the flesh may still produce acts of merciful service, but with much different results.

The person with the motivational gift of mercy who is walking in the flesh can easily lose sight of the church's primary responsibility: "Go and make disciples of all nations" (Matt. 28:19). A person with the mercy gift who serves in church leadership, for example, might be led by the flesh to resist any kingdom-advancing ministry idea that diverts financial resources away from ministries of mercy.

So great are the physical needs in most of our communities, and so in touch with those needs are those with the mercy gift, that their ministry vision can narrow exclusively to those needs. The mercy gift walking in the Spirit has a healthy, well-rounded view of the role of Christ's church in the world. The mercy gift operating in the flesh, however, can lose sight of the bigger picture and demand that all resources be focused on his personal area of ministry concern.

Another risk for the mercy gift walking in the flesh is cynicism. When walking in the Spirit, the person with this gift radiates great hope, even in the midst of overwhelming need, because he has experienced the mercy of Jesus and desires to share Him with others. When the flesh takes hold, however, this person can quickly become cynical, citing the failings of the church, of government and of people in general as reason to lose all hope. This state of mind can lead to the loss of all joy in serving those in need, focusing attention instead on the deteriorating conditions around the world and feeling increasingly overwhelmed by them. When someone with the motivational gift of mercy begins to experience a sense of hopelessness, an attitude that says "it doesn't matter anyway…things will just keep getting worse," it is likely that the gift is being operated in the flesh.

Perhaps the most surprising "dark side" characteristic of the mercy gift is a hardening of the heart. Though this trait is almost the polar opposite of the mercy gift operating in the Spirit, it is nonetheless a risk for those walking in the flesh. The person with the mercy gift will be constantly engaged in serving the poor and afflicted. One reason they have such impact on those they serve is their genuine love and compassion for each person served. This compassion is quite genuine; the mercy gift experiences a heartfelt pain when interacting with someone who is suffering or in need.

However, once the flesh takes hold, the personal engagement will cease, leaving the mercy gift to simply go through the motions of serving but with an emotional detachment. Like so many fast-food restaurants, the person being served is reduced to being a number instead of a name.

Perhaps this happens as a defense mechanism; it isn't fun to experience other people's pain and suffering, and the flesh is only concerned with self. In any case, if you have the mercy gift, beware of your flesh's desire to disengage your emotions from your work, thus stripping from your gift the compassion that makes it effective.

Summarizing the Gift of Mercy

It is important to remember that the Greek word for mercy in Romans 12:8 connotes both *feeling* compassion toward those in need and *acting* on those feelings by demonstrating mercy. To discern whether you have the gift of mercy, look beyond the initial feelings of pity or compassion you experience when encountering someone in need; consider whether those feelings consistently compel you to take action.

Those with the mercy gift feel exceptional empathy and compassion for those who are suffering. Whether the needs are physical, mental, emotional or spiritual, the mercy gift has a unique ability to identify the need and help to relieve the suffering. Even in the midst of difficult and unsightly conditions, those with the gift of mercy are able to serve cheerfully and lovingly, always putting the needs of those suffering ahead of their own.

The mercy gift sees all people as equal and worthy of help. They treat people with love, grace and dignity, physically demonstrating the love of Christ. They seek to bear the burdens of others, serving with gentleness, sensitivity and kindness. Few are able to consistently manifest the love, mercy and compassion of Jesus Christ as readily as those with this motivational gift.

Does your heart break when you drive past a homeless person in your city? Are you deeply grieved by the plight of the poor? Would you gladly give away everything you own if it would eliminate the poverty and suffering in the world?

Do your strong feelings of compassion toward those who are suffering frequently move you to become personally involved in acts of mercy? Are the accounts of Jesus that you most closely identify with His acts of healing the crippled, feeding the hungry and loving the outcast? Do folks who are suffering and in need tend to respond to your sacrificial love? Do those around you refer to you as being empathetic, caring, compassionate and kind? If so, rejoice and give thanks that you have been supernaturally endowed by God with the motivational gift of mercy.

CHAPTER SIXTEEN

Common Misperceptions

"Now about spiritual gifts, brothers, I do not want you to be ignorant."

1 CORINTHIANS 12:1

We are just about to the point of discussing a step-by-step process that will help each of us discern our motivational gift. I'm hopeful that the description of each gift in the preceding chapters has at least helped you to narrow the possibilities; you've most likely been able to eliminate three or four of the gifts as being a match. At this point I thought it would be helpful to offer a few words of caution, which, if ignored, could make it much more difficult to finally determine which motivational gift God has given you.

We've already addressed the most significant misperception regarding spiritual gifts: failure to recognize the three different groupings outlined in the Bible—gifts of the Father (motivational), gifts of the Son (ministry) and gifts of the Spirit (manifestation). Once we've distinguished among these groupings and understood there is only one group that is a permanent endowment by God the Father—those we are to "fan into flame" (2 Tim. 1:6), we must take care to avoid several other traps that can hinder our ability to properly identify our motivational gift.

Misperception #1: Confusing External Factors with Motivational Gifting

As has been discussed in the earlier chapters, we must be careful not to jump to conclusions about motivational gifting simply by observing external behavior, i.e. personality, vocation or natural talent. Your motivational gift is, first and foremost, an inner working of God the Father. Remember the Greek word *energema* from 1 Corinthians 12:6, which indicates an internal operation (or energy) of the Father in the life of each believer. This word can be translated as: working, effects, activities or operation. Although your motivational gift, once it's identified, developed and fanned into flame, will most certainly be demonstrated by corresponding external behavior, it is most readily identified initially by focusing on the internals. Ask yourself, what needs in the body of Christ am I most passionate about? What kind of ministry service makes me come alive?

When I first sought to learn what my own motivational gift was, I immediately fell into the trap of judging by external factors. I listened to some initial teaching on the seven gifts and concluded that I must have the gift of leadership. The reason was that I frequently ended up in charge—formally or informally—of whatever ministry, both in the local church and outside it, that I became involved in. Further, I added to my thought process my secular employment experience. Over the years and in the various companies I worked for, I always ended up in a management position. On the surface, I couldn't identify with any of the spiritual gifts except leadership.

At that point I decided to fan into flame my assumed gift of leadership by serving only in ministry positions consistent with that gifting. As you know if you've served in local church ministry, there is always a wide variety of ministry opportunities available, many desperate for volunteers. I realized that most volunteers burn out over time because they serve in areas incompatible with their God-given gift. I began saying no to all opportunities that didn't appear to fit with the leadership gift.

Unexpectedly and much to my dismay, I started to burn out very quickly. I would sit in leadership meetings for hours on end, wondering why I was there, and then get home exhausted and unmotivated. I would lie awake at night asking God why my ministry service had become so grueling, especially if He had gifted me specifically for this type of work. I began to lose passion for the mission, not because the Great Commission didn't matter to me, but because I felt like I was making no contribution to its fulfillment. I was spending many hours serving in Christ's church but finding no joy in my service. Nor did my service appear to be bearing fruit.

Then, as if by accident, I started getting regular opportunities to teach adult Sunday school. I thought I accepted the offers because it was a fit with the leadership gift, but something happened inside me when I got to teach God's Word—something that absolutely never happened as a leader. I came alive. My times of preparation to teach, hours spent intensely studying the Bible, were filled with joy and excitement. Even though I usually felt nervous about delivering the lesson, I was excited to share with others what I felt God had taught me that week. When the time came to present the lesson, there was an internal passion and joy that I had not experienced in any other type of ministry.

I didn't realize at the time that I had misinterpreted my motivational gift by focusing on the externals. I continued in various leadership roles, all the while wondering why teaching was so much more fun than leading. It wasn't until I had the opportunity to teach on spiritual gifts that it all came together. My wife was reviewing my list of characteristics for the various gifts. When she got to a particular gift, her silent reading was interrupted by an excited, "This is you!"

Lori, who knows me as well as (maybe better than) I know myself, was immediately able to identify my motivational gift. Why? Because she lived with it. She watched for years as I was drained, physically and emotionally, by various leadership positions, and she experienced with me the intense joy of losing myself in God's Word for hours at a time, longing to be taught by God in order that I might teach others.

It was interesting to then go back and review my experiences in every ministry I had ever been involved in since coming to faith in Christ. I did an honest assessment of each, scoring them based on such things as how much I enjoyed the work, whether there was affirmation from others, and whether the service bore any fruit. This was an eye-opening experience. Every ministry that had to do with helping others to learn God's Word and grow deeper in their relationship with Him had the highest scores in all categories. All leadership work I had done that was unrelated to teaching His Word lagged far behind.

I share this experience only in hopes of encouraging you as you seek to discern your gift. As you went through this book, you might not have identified with any of the seven motivational gifts. If so, take heart. The problem is not that you don't have a motivational gift; the problem is that you've not yet served in a ministry that is compatible with your gifting. If you've served in various church ministries but have not yet experienced a sense of passion, fruit or fulfillment, ask yourself how you ended up in those ministries in the first place. Most recruiting in the local church is based on what I call the "warm body" theory. When someone in charge of a ministry needs additional volunteers, the ideal person to fill each position becomes simply any warm body. Recruiting is done with absolutely no regard to gifting, which is why ministry leaders spend most of their time trying to recruit new warm bodies into positions continually vacated by burned-out warm bodies.

Ministry leaders who do venture beyond the warm body theory in recruiting almost always default to focusing on external factors. Need someone to teach the seven- and eight-year-old Sunday school class? Find a church member who teaches elementary school. Need someone to head up the outreach committee? Find the person with the most outgoing personality. Need people to cook for the pancake breakfast, serve at a homeless shelter, or fill a spot on the committee or board charged with caring for the church's physical plant? Do we have any chefs, social workers or carpenters in our congregation to fill those respective positions?

I cannot overstate the importance of first examining internal passion when trying to identify your own motivational gift or when recruiting others into a ministry position. There are times when the external factors will actually argue *against* putting a gifted person in the right position. Take teaching, for example. Many folks are frightened to death to stand and speak in front of an audience. Many others have never had the opportunity to try it. Compare someone who is afraid of public speaking, or someone with no experience, to the person whose vocation has for years required public speeches and leading group presentations. Who is more likely to be recruited by the church to teach adult Sunday school?

Remember that motivational gifting is not likely to be polished externally until it has had time to develop (is "fanned into flame"). There are many profoundly gifted teachers in the body of Christ whose public speaking ability, when judged purely on the externals, pales in comparison to those more polished and experienced in public speaking. Some gifted teachers are more effective in one-on-one discipleship or leading a very small group than standing before a congregation. Some would rather write books and Bible study outlines than stand before a group at all. The emphasis must be on the internal drive and passion the teacher feels while actually serving. It may take months or years for someone with the teaching gift to become completely comfortable teaching in front of a large group, especially if there is no prior experience in this area, but the internal compulsion to teach God's Word will be evident from the beginning. This will be true of all of the motivational gifts.

Misperception #2:
Confusing Sanctified Behavior with Motivational Gifting

One of the glorious promises of God is that every Christian is being "conformed to the image of His Son" (Rom. 8:29 NASB). John states in his first epistle a related, almost incomprehensible truth: "But we know that when he appears, we shall be like him" (1 John 3:2). Over the years of our walk with Jesus, His Spirit is powerfully at work in us conforming us to His image, so much so that we will actually be like Him when we finally see Him. This process is called sanctification.

I noted earlier that I believe Jesus demonstrated all seven of the motivational gifts, examples of which are given in each individual chapter describing a particular gift. Since each of us is being conformed to the image of Christ, it follows that we will necessarily grow in our demonstration of Christlike behaviors.

For example, before I was saved and therefore indwelt by the Holy Spirit, I had no interest in giving money away. Since coming to faith in Christ and maturing over time, I find it an increasingly joyful experience to contribute money to advancing the kingdom of God. This is not because I have the motivational gift of giving but because I'm being sanctified.

All of us who follow Christ will inevitably grow in the seven areas we've identified as the motivational gifts. Those who've never been interested in teaching will inevitably find themselves sharing God's Word with others. Those who've never been particularly sympathetic will increasingly find themselves more readily offering words of encouragement. This should be expected: The very behaviors Jesus displayed should become increasingly evident in the life of every believer.

When John the Baptist, imprisoned and facing death, sent his disciples to ask Jesus if He was the Messiah, Jesus replied: "Go back and report to John what you hear and see: The blind receive sight, the lame walk, those who have leprosy are cured, the deaf hear, the dead are raised, and the good news is preached to the poor" (Matt. 11:4–5). Jesus pointed to the fruit of His works as evidence that He was indeed the promised Messiah.

Similarly, Christians should be increasingly able to point to their works as evidence of their identification as Jesus' disciples. We should expect that the formerly unmerciful will show mercy, the shy will boldly proclaim God's truth, the stingy will give cheerfully and the most non-confrontational of Christians will confront and rebuke blatant sin. While this is a truth to be rejoiced in and embraced, we must be careful not to confuse our sanctified behavior with our motivational gifting.

In order to distinguish between motivational gifting and sanctified behavior, I would point again to what you are experiencing internally. I know several people with the motivational gift of giving, and I can honestly say that I've never experienced the deep level of joy in giving to God's work that they do. As noted above, I find it enjoyable to give, more so each year that I walk with Christ. I began giving purely out of obedience; now I would give to God's work even if I were not commanded to do so. I would continue to give and I would find fulfillment in doing so. But the joy I experience in giving, or with serving or showing mercy, cannot be compared with what happens in my heart when I get to teach God's Word.

You may have resonated with several of the motivational gifts as you read the descriptions. Most folks going through this study will be able to quickly eliminate several of the motivational gifts from consideration, but there are usually two or three that remain as possibilities. In making our final determination it is important to distinguish between sanctified behavior, which is a characteristic of every Christian, and motivational gifting. We need to analyze not just changes in our behavior since coming to faith in Christ, but also our deepest heart response to each ministry service we've experienced.

Misperception #3: Confusing Manifestation and Ministry Gifts with Motivational Gifting

As noted at the beginning of this book, one of the reasons there is so much confusion about spiritual gifts is that many teachers lump them all together; no distinction is made between gifts of the Father, Son and Spirit. When the motivational gifts that we are commanded to fan into flame are not separated from the other gifts, two things will happen that hinder our growth.

First, we'll focus on a manifestation gift that we've experienced, or a ministry that we've chosen to pursue, and believe we've identified our gift, leaving us with no idea—or intention of pursing—the one motivational gift with which the Father has endowed us.

Second, since we will have experienced more than one manifestation gift and served in more than one ministry, we'll wrongly conclude that there is no single spiritual gift that we can focus on developing.

Ask any group of Christians if they know their spiritual gift and most will be confused and unsure. Some will have absolutely no idea, while others will name a number of different gifts as possibilities. Rarely will someone definitively state a single motivational gift that drives their ministry service.

Interestingly, on the rare occasions that a Christian will claim one particular gift, it will usually be something that is either not a spiritual gift at all or not in the category of motivational gifts. The challenge with wrongly identifying your gift is that you'll never know the passion and joy—or see the abundant fruit—God intended for you when He gave you this precious gift. The challenge with identifying with several spiritual gifts is the inability to develop the single gift, to fan it into flame as God has commanded.

If you had no idea of your spiritual gifting when you began reading this book, you were somewhat blessed in that you had a clean slate to work with. If you had already identified several gifts as your own, that may have biased your reading and made it more difficult to identify a single motivational gift. The issue is not whether more than one gift will be manifested in the life of a Christian; we've acknowledged that manifestation gifts of the Holy Spirit will come and go as He determines, and that we are free to pursue any of the ministries in the church at our discretion.

The key is not to become confused by these two entirely different categories of gifts and miss the single, motivational gift that is permanent and enduring. Focusing on the wrong gift will inevitably lead to neglecting the right one; focusing on a gift that is completely under the control of the Holy Spirit will keep us from fanning into flame the one gift we exercise control over.

Therefore, my suggestion for avoiding this misperception is to properly distinguish between the three gift groupings. Rejoice in any and every manifestation of the Holy Spirit you've experienced in your life; give thanks and praise to the Son for allowing you to volunteer in the service areas of your choice, whether formal offices (i.e., pastor, teacher, evangelist) or lay ministries. But when it comes to identifying that one gift, the inner working of God the Father that we've referred to as your motivational gift, look only to the list of gifts that represent direct operations of God. Only then will you be able to discern the special endowment He has given you; only then will you experience the abundant blessing He intends for your service.

Potential for Conflict

If you are able to avoid these common misperceptions as you go through the process of motivational gift discernment, you will find it much easier to accurately identify your gift. I would like to offer a final piece of advice that is applicable to all who are successful in discerning and exercising their motivational gift: Be aware of the potential for ministry conflict, especially with those who have not understood their personal gifting.

Knowing your gift should enable you to appreciate and celebrate the unique differences between your perspective and that of others with whom you serve in ministry. Too often, however, in the exercise of our gift we are prone to become narrow in our thinking and unyielding in our opinions. Let me explain.

Suppose the pastors and officers in a local church are meeting to discuss whether to initiate a capital campaign in order to expand the size of the sanctuary and add classroom space. All the leaders are in agreement that the church is bursting at the seams and something needs to be done. The pastor is visionary in his thinking and approach to ministry. He has called this meeting in order to propose the capital campaign. What begins as a relatively calm discussion soon erupts into a full-scale argument. By the end of the evening—four hours after the meeting began—this beaten and emotionally drained group walks slowly to the parking lot trying to figure out what just happened. Nothing was decided and no one is quite sure they want to continue the discussion. What happened? The motivational gifts collided.

The first person to object to raising money—millions of dollars, in fact—to expand the sanctuary was the team member with the motivational gift of mercy. "How can we even think about spending millions of dollars of God's money to make ourselves more comfortable when there are thousands of people living in poverty, including hundreds of homeless, within ten miles of this church?"

The gift of prophecy, face turning red and trying unsuccessfully to control the hint of sarcasm in his voice, speaks next. "If I'm not mistaken, it was Jesus who said, 'The poor you will always have among you.' We could sell this building and give all the proceeds—as well as the money we have in the bank—to the poor and we wouldn't begin to eradicate poverty in this community. This church isn't here to preach a social gospel; the only hope for a lost and dying world is the Gospel of Jesus Christ. And if we keep turning our unsaved neighbors away every Sunday because we refuse to make room for them, then we've failed in our mission no matter how many hungry mouths we feed."

It is at this point that the gift of encouragement tries to play peacemaker. "Come on, brothers, let's not raise our voices. I think your passion for the poor is admirable, Bill. And I've always appreciated your consistent focus on the mission of Christ's church, Tom. But we need to be sure we're acting with honor and respect toward one another, even when we disagree about something as important as this."

It takes every ounce of self-control the prophet can muster to keep his thoughts to himself: *If this guy weren't so touchy-feely and wishy-washy, maybe he'd be capable of making a decision!*

Before long the leadership gift has laid out—in rapid succession—all the steps that need to be taken for a successful capital campaign, including what volunteer positions need to be filled, how long it will take to raise the funds, the approximate amount needed to be raised and the details of the kick-off dinner for the congregation. Not surprisingly, he personally volunteers to chair the committee.

The gift of giving excitedly joins the conversation at this point, excited at the thought of coordinating a stewardship campaign and pledging to give sacrificially to the building fund.

"Wait a minute," pleads the mercy gift. "I thought this is only in the discussion phase. You guys are making it sound as if we've already approved it."

The teaching gift quickly chimes in, "Well, you know what God says: 'If we set out to build a tower we must first count the cost, lest we get started and not have sufficient funds to complete the work.' I say we shouldn't even be having this discussion until we know exactly how much money we're talking about. I suggest we table this discussion until we're better prepared for it."

The pastor buries his head in his hands; the prophet stands up and walks around, trying to keep his composure. The leader wonders silently why something so simple to achieve as a multi-million dollar capital campaign is causing so much strife.

The gift of service has been tuning in and out of this discussion and offers no opinion, distracted instead by making and serving coffee to everyone and tidying up the meeting room so no one else will have to stay late.

As you can imagine, putting several different motivational gifts in the same room and asking them to make an important decision can produce serious conflict, even broken relationships. I point this out so we can all see the vital necessity of understanding—and appreciating—the other motivational gifts. The prophet wouldn't get frustrated with the mercy gift if he took time to understand and appreciate his perspective. In fact, he would realize how crucial the mercy gift's perspective is. The teacher wouldn't be frustrated with the visionary nature of the leader and prophet, who are always ready to go forward without first "counting the cost," but rather would appreciate the differences in their perspective.

A ministry team that fails to understand, appreciate—even celebrate—the vast differences in perspective that result from the various motivational gifts will eventually implode. We must understand, as Paul encouraged the church at Corinth:

> The body is a unit, though it is made up of many parts; and though all its parts are many, they form one body...But in fact God has arranged the parts in the body, every one of them, just as he wanted them to be. (1 Cor. 12:12, 18)

The relevant question for those of us serving on ministry teams is: Do we believe God? If we believe that God is the giver of these gifts, and that He has purposely arranged them "just as he wanted them to be," ought we not to appreciate the gift of another as much as we appreciate our own? "The eye cannot say to the hand, 'I don't need you!'" (1 Cor. 12:21).

As one who has the gift of teaching, I very much want to learn the perspective of others on my ministry team before making a decision. Why? Because I have a narrow perspective, limited by the natural bias of my own gifting. I might never stop to think about the impact a decision might have on the poor if not for the honest opinion being shared by my sister with the gift of mercy. I could scarcely conceive our church body's ability to give sacrificially toward a major ministry project without the encouragement of my brother with the gift of giving.

When the various gifts come together in joint ministry service, there is great potential for conflict. It is imperative that we learn not just to tolerate the other gifts but also to realize how much we need them. The well-balanced church is the one that has all of the motivational gifts active in ministry leadership and service. Let us never fail to appreciate the other gifts, or begin to take them for granted. Rather, let us celebrate the beauty of all of the gifts working in harmony as God intended.

CHAPTER SEVENTEEN

Discerning Your Motivational Gift

"We have different gifts, according to the grace given us."

ROMANS 12:6

I can think of at least seven steps that are very helpful in the process of discerning your motivational gift. Some who are reading might not feel the need to go through this process; you knew which motivational gift God has given you as soon as you read the description of it. For those who aren't yet sure, or who would like an objective process to confirm your conclusion, I offer the following:

STEP ONE: PRAY

The first—and most important—step in seeking to discern your gift is to ask God. One of my favorite verses in all of the Bible is James 1:5:

> If any of you lacks wisdom, he should ask God, who gives generously to all without finding fault, and **it will be given to him** (emphasis mine).

If we understand that God has graciously endowed each of us with a specific gift, one that represents His own, direct working inside of us, should we not earnestly desire to know what that gift is? And when God's child approaches Him in prayer asking for wisdom to know what gift He has bestowed, could we possibly think our loving Father would withhold that information? This verse is God's promise to give us wisdom when we ask Him.

Consider also the fact that God has commanded us to "not neglect" and "fan into flame" the gift He has blessed us with. Such a command could not be obeyed were we unable (or unwilling) to discern the gift He has given us. Whether you have abundant experience with prayer or are a new Christian just learning about communication with your loving Father, go directly to Him, immediately and regularly, asking Him to reveal to you the special gift He has given you. He will hear you, and He will most certainly answer.

STEP TWO: STUDY

As we commit to pray for God's wisdom and for discernment on a particular topic relating to our faith, it is important that we are also studying what His Word teaches us about that topic. Whether we want to learn about worship, finance, evangelism or the Christian life in general, our source for accurate information is always the Bible. During this process of seeking to discern our motivational gift, it is vitally important that we search the Scriptures to increase our understanding of this important aspect of our Christian life.

This book is an attempt to help you do that, but no book is a substitute for directly reading and studying God's Word. I have cited many verses and passages throughout this book that relate to the topic of spiritual gifts. I would highly recommend that each of us spend private time before the Lord, meditating on some of these passages as we pray for wisdom and understanding. God speaks to us through His Word.

STEP THREE: TEST

The more ministry experience you've had in the past, the easier it will be to discern your motivational gift. That is, assuming you have been able to serve in a ministry area compatible with your gifting. But whether you already have a sense of your gift and simply need confirmation—or you have no idea which gift God has given you—the third step is to test different ministries to see if they fit.

I'm not sure it is possible to know with certainty your motivational gift until you've tested that area and felt the joy and passion that accompany the gift.

Testing new ministries can be very difficult in the local church for a reason I alluded to earlier: too many open spots, too few volunteers. We are often reluctant to volunteer to test a ministry because our experience has taught us that all service is presumed to be perpetual, that once you volunteer for a ministry it can be next to impossible to terminate your involvement.

For that reason, we may need to be very direct with the ministry leader we're serving under, letting him know we aren't sure we're a fit for the ministry but would be willing to volunteer on a trial basis. Make a commitment upfront for only a specified period of time.

A short-term initial commitment is important because, even if you are enjoying the ministry, you will still need to test several others before you can be sure you've correctly identified your gift. This is especially true if you have the gift of service, in which case you'll love just about every ministry you're assigned to. My point is that testing is only effective when you have various ministry experiences to compare and contrast.

Don't allow yourself to languish in an ill-fitting ministry because of guilt. If you are in a church that regularly teaches on spiritual gifts and tries to match ministry service with gifting, the ministry leader will understand when you suggest a short-term trial.

However, if this is a foreign concept in your church—as it seems to be for most—I have two suggestions: 1. be clear upfront in setting the terms, and 2. be firm when the term has expired.

Be prepared for the inevitable "But what about the children?" when your term expires in the nursery, or the concerned "I guess some people will just have to go hungry" when it is time to leave the food pantry. It is unfortunate that this method of recruiting and retaining volunteers has become so typical in the church. In any case, better to be prepared going in than to risk failing to discern your motivational gift because guilt kept you from changing ministries.

A final suggestion with regard to this step: Test early and often. The less certain you are going in as to which gift you have, the longer the period of testing will be. Hang in there! Keep testing; serve in as many areas as you can and try to make sure they are different from each other. If you go from leading the capital campaign to leading the deacon board to leading your church's small groups ministry, I might suggest you haven't actually tested three different areas of service but only one. Try leading a ministry if you feel like that might be your gift, but also spend time teaching and serving in a mercy ministry. Try to get exposure to as many areas as possible. This is much easier, of course, if you've already been able to narrow the list of gifts to just two or three possible matches. In any case, the best way to discern with certainty your motivational gift is to test it in actual ministry.

Step Four: Examine

This step is critical during the process of testing new ministries. As you are serving, constantly examine how you are feeling about the service, both while you are there and when you're away from it. This step is focused on assessing your internal passion and joy. Is the ministry service life-giving or life-draining? When you're away from the ministry, do you find your mind constantly drifting back to the experience with an accompanying joy and fulfillment? Do you find yourself excitedly thinking of ways you can improve the ministry or your personal involvement in it? Do you think about those being served in the ministry—even find yourself moved to pray for them during periods between serving in that area?

It is vitally important that you are examining your thoughts, feelings and even motives during your time of service in each ministry. When you are serving in an area compatible with your motivational gift, that experience will feel decidedly different than all other ministry service. Though it may only be a small flame in the beginning—think of the flame in the fireplace when the logs are first lit versus the roaring fire thirty minutes later—it will be unmistakable. By proper examination in the beginning, you'll be able to quickly discern your gift and then enjoy the blessed process of fanning it to flame.

Step Five: Evaluate

This may seem similar to step four, but the evaluation process focuses more on seeking external affirmation than examining internal experience. Honestly assess whether you are good at the particular ministry. Does it come easily to you? How do others respond to your service? Are your efforts bearing fruit?

Be sure not to apply this step in isolation; it is most valuable when done as part of the entire process. I noted earlier that being good at something isn't necessarily an indicator of spiritual giftedness. Someone with experience in public speaking may do very well teaching adult Sunday school but may find the work tedious and draining.

This fifth step is just a further way of affirming your gift once you think you've discerned what it is. God has provided motivational gifts for the building up of the body of Christ and the advancement of His kingdom. If we are developing and applying the motivational gift He has specifically chosen to endow us with, we should expect to bear fruit in the exercise of that gift.

When we are operating within our giftedness we are not the only ones who are blessed. We must remember that our gift was not given to us exclusively for our own benefit but for the body of Christ. Others will be edified when we exercise our motivational gift, and there will almost certainly be some external affirmation. The fruit that is borne by the exercise of our gift will not be hidden. We need to be willing to honestly evaluate the existence—or non-existence—of external affirmation and ministry fruit.

Step Six: Counsel

This step is important in many areas of life, and particularly so when we are trying to discern our motivational gift. I am a strong believer that "many advisers make victory sure" (Prov. 11:14). During the process of discerning our motivational gift it is wise to seek counsel from one or more mature Christians who know us well and love us enough to be honest.

I usually prefer for counsel to be sought at the very beginning of a spiritual process, but in this case I would suggest going through the other steps first. The reason is that a counselor can help primarily with external affirmation—whether or not you're good at something, how others are responding to you, if your ministry is bearing fruit—as opposed to being able to see what is going on in your heart.

Of course, if the counselor is someone very close to you, such as a spouse, close friend or ministry partner, he or she will also have a sense of your internal experience. If you're blessed to have such relationships I would encourage you to engage these folks from the beginning of the process. Ask them to review the seven motivational gifts and to let you know if they have a sense of how God has gifted you. Their initial counsel will not be definitive. You'll still need to go through this process, but they may be able to help narrow the list with you.

In many cases, however, the mature Christian you seek counsel from won't be able to judge the internals, so you'll need to sort through those steps on your own. Let me just encourage you that somewhere along the way in your discernment process, it is wise and helpful to seek counsel.

STEP SEVEN: AFFIRM

This seventh step is not actually a part of the process to discern your motivational gift, but rather what you should do once you've identified it. One characteristic of the Christian life is humility, and we often tend to misinterpret humility to mean believing that we are not good at anything. Acknowledging strength, victory or success in any area, we fear, might be construed as arrogant and prideful—not qualities we strive for as followers of Christ. Remember, however, that when we acknowledge and affirm our motivational gift, it is not ourselves we give glory to. How could it be? This gift is by its very nature an operation of God in our lives.

Affirming and rejoicing in the motivational gift God has blessed us with is no more self-centered, nor is it less glorifying to Him, than rejoicing in the salvation He has granted us. God's forgiveness of our sins and His promise of eternal life through Jesus are absolute. When I affirm my assurance of salvation I am not affirming myself. How could I be arrogant about something I didn't earn, don't deserve, and couldn't have embraced if not for the Holy Spirit? How could I maintain it if it were not already permanently maintained by Jesus Himself? Am I lacking in humility to acknowledge—indeed to rejoice in—this precious gift? I would propose that it is our Father, the One who bestowed the gift, who is glorified, both in its acknowledgement and its exercise.

I include this seventh step only to encourage you that once you've prayerfully identified, tested and affirmed your motivational gift, you be willing to acknowledge the gift both before God and before men. If your church leadership isn't providing the opportunity for you to contribute to church life by exercising your gift, let them know what your gift is and ask them to dispatch you to a suitable ministry.

Just as important, if you are asked to serve in a ministry area incompatible with your gift, be equally honest. "Thanks for asking. I've found that my spiritual gift is teaching so that's where I've been volunteering my time. I've never been very good at mercy ministries, but I think it is a critical area for us and I'll commit to praying that God will quickly bring the right person along. If I can think of anyone that might be a good fit, I'll be sure to let you know." Even the most aggressive recruiters will accept that explanation, and there isn't a hint of arrogance in it.

We will always be asked to serve in ministries that we're not suited for, simply because there are so many openings in the typical church. But when I accept a position for which I'm not gifted, not only does the ministry suffer but I'm also taking a spot away from the person who is gifted.

God provides all of the gifts in His church and we have to trust that He has already prepared someone when a ministry spot is open. If church leaders are having trouble finding the right people to serve, it is most likely because they are not training the congregation in the area of spiritual gifts. If God would have a specific ministry exist in a church, He will indeed provide the gifts necessary for the successful execution of that ministry.

A Plea to Pastors

There is a reason that many churches are reluctant to teach about spiritual gifts. Considering the numerous open positions in local church ministries—and the increasing challenge of finding volunteers to fill these positions—it is no wonder pastors might be concerned about teaching on spiritual gifts. Why? Because then everyone in the congregation will have another ready-made excuse to add to the arsenal of reasons why they can't serve in a particular ministry. "That's not my gift" sounds eerily like "that's not my job," frightening words for the pastor who is called to lead an army of volunteers. I can sympathize with this concern; it is hard enough already to recruit busy people into ministry service.

I truly believe, however, that it is a lack of solid teaching about spiritual gifts that has led to the current shortage of volunteers. Most church members have willingly served at least once or twice when asked by ministry leaders. The problem was that no one helped them assess their giftedness before directing them to a ministry, and no one walked with them along the way to help them evaluate their experience.

Since most ministry assignments end up being based on random selection, it stands to reason that most people's first ministry experience is in an area not compatible with their motivational gift. In fact, the odds are six out of seven that this first experience will not be a fit.

Then it gets worse. As this willing volunteer becomes drained by ineffective and unfruitful service, she tries talking to the ministry leader about her experience, hoping for a caring ear and the encouragement to move on to a better ministry fit. Instead, she is made to feel guilty, reminded that there is a shortage of volunteers because everyone keeps dropping out after making a commitment. And so the volunteer languishes until she can find either an acceptable excuse for leaving the ministry or some unsuspecting new church member she can convince to replace her. (See the section about my "warm body" theory.)

After one or two such ministry experiences, one thing becomes certain: this volunteer is highly unlikely ever to offer to serve again. How tragic. I wonder how many gifted teachers are sitting in our pews, feeling disengaged from the church's ministry but afraid to volunteer again because of a bad experience as a trustee.

Or how many folks with the gift of mercy are shriveling on the vine in suburban churches because there is no ministry to the inner city needy. Or how many with the gift of encouragement, who would most certainly excel in a counseling or bereavement ministry, are relegated to pew-sitting because of a draining experience chairing the missions committee, followed by a heavy dose of guilt when they sought to step down from this ill-fitting assignment.

Consider the alternative: an army of gifted servants of Christ, educated in the area of spiritual gifts and mentored through the process of motivational gift discernment. Will such a group not enthusiastically seek to deploy their respective gifts? They will not need to be pressured to serve. They'll serve without tiring because they'll be doing what God created them to do. A Christian who has identified his motivational gift and has experienced the deep joy and passion that accompany the exercise of this gift, will spend the rest of his life enthusiastically serving the church of Jesus Christ.

A Plea to Church Members

I would be remiss to close this book without also acknowledging an important reality of life in Christ's church: Sometimes there is important ministry work to be done and we might not always have the luxury, especially in a new or growing church, to confine our service to areas compatible with our motivational gift. In a new church plant, for example, everyone in the core group will need to wear multiple hats, at least until the congregation grows and can be trained. Although the absolute ideal is for every church member to be actively engaged in ministry compatible with his or her motivational gift, there are times when the church's mission takes precedence over this ideal. Short-term sacrifice for long-term gain.

We who are servants in Christ's church must be willing to do whatever is necessary to advance the cause of Christ in our church, community and the world. That said, however, we must also insist that our churches are faithful in educating us with regard to spiritual gifts, that we are mentored through the process of discerning our gift and then dispatched to ministry service compatible with that gift.

Just as a church that refuses to teach on biblical stewardship has no right to complain about a lack of giving, so the church that fails to teach about spiritual gifts cannot complain about a lack of motivated volunteers.

If your church is newly planted, going through a growth spurt or is made up of a high percentage of new converts, be willing to wear several ministry hats, including some that might not fit very well. At the same time, encourage your pastor to train church members in the area of spiritual gifts so that each ministry position is eventually filled by a suitably gifted volunteer.

IN CLOSING ...

It is my earnest prayer that you will be able to discern your motivational gift. It will be an incredible blessing and encouragement to me if God should use this book to assist you in the process. If you still haven't been able to discern with certainty which gift God has given you, please commit to working through the seven steps listed in this chapter. God has given you a motivational gift for a reason. He wants and expects you to discern your gift and to fan it into flame. Countless lives will be impacted for Christ as a result of your diligence and perseverance.

Once you've discerned the motivational gift that God the Father has blessed you with, rejoice and give thanks. Then move ahead on this wonderful journey of exercising His gift, for the glory of God and the advancement of Christ's church. Your life will never be the same!

"Now you are the body of Christ, and each one of you is a part of it."

1 CORINTHIANS 12:27